D0723565

The Himalayas

A Syllabus of the Region's History, Anthropology, and Religion

THE HIMALAYAS

A SYLLABUS OF THE REGION'S HISTORY, ANTHROPOLOGY, AND RELIGION

Todd T. Lewis

Theodore Riccardi, Jr.

Foreword by Gerald D. Berreman

Published as an Occasional Paper by the Association for Asian Studies, Inc.

© 1995 by the Association for Asian Studies

All Rights Reserved. Written permission must be secured from the publisher to use or reproduce any part of this book.

Published by the Association for Asian Studies, Inc.
1 Lane Hall
The University of Michigan
204 South State Street
Ann Arbor, Michigan 48104

Library of Congress Cataloging-in-Publication Data

Lewis, Todd Thornton, 1952–
        The Himalayas: a syllabus of the region's history, anthropology, and religion/Todd T. Lewis, Theodore Riccardi, Jr.; foreword by Gerald D. Berreman.
        p.cm.—(Association for Asian Studies Occasional Papers Series)
        Includes bibliographical references.
        ISBN 0-924304-34-0

        1. Himalaya Mountains Region—History. 2. Ethnology—Himalaya Mountains Region. 3. Himalaya Mountains Region—Religion.
I. Riccardi, Theodore. II.Title. III. Series: Occasional Papers Series (Association for Asian Studies)

DS485.H6L48 1995   95-24655
954.96—dc20   CIP

The printing of this volume has been financed from a revolving fund, supported in part by the Luce Foundation.

Printed in the United States of America on acid-free, archival quality paper.

TABLE OF CONTENTS

LIST OF MAPS

PHOTOGRAPHIC CREDITS

Richard English: 24, 31b, 32, 65, 162, 223
David Sassoon: 39
Mark Kenoyer: 126b
Theodore Riccardi, Jr: x, 3, 14, 26, 47, 48, 59, 66, 77, 92, 107, 130, 180
Todd Lewis: 4, 13, 31a, 35, 40, 46, 115, 125, 126a, 132, 144, 146, 158, 161, 165, 166, 177,
    178, 179, 187, 189, 191, 202, 204, 208, 211, 225, 228, 230, 232, 233, 234, 236, 238, 240
National Anthropological Archives, Smithsonian Institution: 36, 78, 88, 108, 192, 201, 207,
    212, 220, 222

FOREWORD

The magnitude, incisiveness, and importance of the work that has gone into this comprehensive volume probably cannot be fully appreciated by anyone who has not attempted to teach a course on the peoples and cultures of the Himalayas. There is scarcely a region in the world of comparable extent -- be it surface (including vertical) area, or limited to a horizontal area -- that can compare in cultural diversity, historical complexity, and religious variety with what has been called the Indo-Tibetan interface, the Himalayan frontier, or simply the Himalayan region. Few areas, too, have been subjected to such intensive ethnological scrutiny in so short a time as has the Nepalese portion of the region, beginning in the mid-1950's when Nepal first became accessible to contemporary scholars. In the adjacent Indian Himalayas the quantity of contemporary scholarly research has been less, but has extended over a longer time span up to the present by Indian and foreign scholars, many associated with the Anthropological Survey of India.

For the researcher, teacher or student of matters Himalayan, the present volume is of unprecedented and unparalleled value, for it draws upon information from all of these sources and many others, including the most recent, as well as on its authors' own research and experience.

The publication and consequent ready availability of this syllabus will surely bring it the attention it deserves -- and its author-editors the appreciation they have earned -- among Himalayanists, anthropologists, comparative religionists, historians and other scholars worldwide. Although it is presented entirely in outline form, that outline is not merely skeletal. It is rich in content and is supplemented with relevant bibliographies for each chapter, bringing together many little-known or hard to find works as well as major sources, all of them carefully selected for their quality and relevance. Among its most useful features are the illuminating maps and charts prepared by Joy Lewis.

No academic course or course-segment on the Himalayas, be it ethnographic, historical, religious, or civilizational in focus, can fail to benefit from the stimulus of the information, organizational structure and references to published sources provided here. None could use them all or in their entirety, but it is by having so many resources available that one can choose and construct one's own course. This is the unique and invaluable contribution of this volume. Those of us who study and teach about the Himalayan peoples -- and all who want to know about them -- are deeply indebted to its authors.

Gerald D. Berreman
University of California, Berkeley

PREFACE

Beginning almost a decade ago, a series of projects was conceived at the Southern Asian Institute, Columbia University, to aid in the teaching of Himalayan studies. At that time the authors produced with Richard English a two-volume anthology entitled *The Himalayas: Essays and Readings*, and with Bruce Owens, *A Bibliography of Himalayan Studies*. This syllabus is the third in the series. Like the *Syllabus of Indian Civilization* devised by Barbara Miller and Leonard Gordon (New York: Columbia University Press, 1971), the authors consider the present work a pedagogical tool, meant for the use of those who teach about the Himalayas or who wish to include something about the Himalayas in other courses. But we hope that it will be of use to others as well -- the student, government servant, or perhaps even the general reader -- who might use it to inform herself about a little-known area of the world.

It should be kept in mind that a syllabus is not a treatise. One cannot read it through and digest it. It is only an outline of important points and illustrative examples, providing talking points for lecturers, reference points for others. For those who already teach courses about the area, it is hoped that it will supplement their teaching, not replace their own efforts. For those wishing to begin to teach such courses, it is hoped that this syllabus will be of sufficient use to facilitate that task. For those who wish merely to learn something of the Himalayas, it is hoped that the outlines and recommended readings will provide enough of interest for them to move beyond it. The syllabus is something to be used, therefore, as one needs.

Here, then, is one view of the peoples and cultures of the Himalayas. It is only one of many possible ways of organizing some of what has been written about the region; the authors would be the last to claim that they have made here anything more than a modest beginning toward a sympathetic understanding of any area of the world that is increasingly contested.

We gratefully acknowledge grants from the U.S. Department of Education that supported this project. A fellowship from the Social Science Research Council assisted in the cartography and funds from the College of the Holy Cross Research and Publication Committee underwrote the preparation of the final manuscript.

We would also like to express our thanks to Ken Scott of the Holy Cross Faculty Computing Center for expertly preparing the camera-ready copy of the manuscript and to Joel Villa of the Holy Cross Audio-Visual Department for ably printing many of the black and white photographs illustrating these pages.

The authors would like to thank Richard English, Bruce Owens, and many others for the discussions out of which it arose. We also wish to thank Joy Chen Lewis for drawing the maps that accompany the work.

Todd Thornton Lewis
Theodore Riccardi, Jr.
May, 1995

Himalayan Entrepot: Asan Tol Bazaar of Kathmandu

INTRODUCTION

Peoples of the Himalayan region live in all of the ways that human beings have devised to survive on the earth: as hunters and gatherers, nomadic herdsmen, shifting slash and burn cultivators, settled agriculturalists, petty traders, and industrial entrepreneurs. They live in felt tents, thatched huts, brick houses, and stucco palaces. Over forty million people live across the terrain dominated by the world's highest mountain range. This frontier region is predominantly rural. Transport and communication are particularly difficult, and the ethnic groups are astoundingly diverse. Isolation and countless migrations have led to myriad forms of social and cultural adaptation. There are Muslims, Hindus, and Buddhists, but many peoples also retain their own separate ethnic identity and worship. This one thousand, five hundred mile long region is the homeland for what is arguably the most diverse spectrum of peoples in the world.

This syllabus presents an overview of the Himalayan region in terms of history, society, and culture. It also attempts to delineate the central socio-cultural processes that have shaped recent Himalayan history. It is divided into five parts: "General Perspectives", "History", "Four Ethno-Geographic Regions", "Major Cultural Centers", and "Continuities in Culture, Religion, and Society." Each chapter is accompanied by a list of recommended readings and references in English.

The chapters of Part I introduce the region from a number of viewpoints. If there is one feature that Himalayan peoples have in common, it is that they live along the frontier between Indic and Tibetan civilizations. For this reason, we begin by considering the characteristics of frontier areas and sketch the historical patterns and socio-cultural processes that have influenced the region from both sides. We then present the general structure of the geographical environment and outline the subsistence patterns that conform to it. Subsequent chapters develop the characteristics of this frontier by emphasizing the networks and political formations that dominated regional societies and cultures: trade and pilgrimage routes, central places and, to use Tambiah's useful term, "galactic polities," and the legacy of modern states. The cultural traditions that Indian and Tibetan peoples articulated regarding the Himalayan region itself round out the topics covered in this section.

In Part II, we have summarized the main points known to date about the three historical centers of Himalayan civilization: Kashmir, Nepal, and Assam. Each emerged as an Indicized culture hearth zone relying on intensive agriculture and regional trade. We have divided the presentation according to three historical epochs -- Ancient (up to 1200 AD), Middle (1200-1800), and Modern (post-1800) and have sought to convey the major socio-cultural facts. Religion, as the predominant focus of texts and inscriptions, figures prominently. The inclusion of Assam in the syllabus may at first glance look anomalous, for Assam is clearly not a mountainous area. But as with Nepal, the eastern Himalayan areas cannot be understood without an account of the history and culture of the lowlands to the south. It is for this reason that Assam, as the continuous area to the mountains, is included.

In Parts III and IV, we identify four ethno-geographic regions and two major cultural centers. This division into ethno-geographic regions does not imply carving out homogeneous regions in sharp relief: to the contrary, it assumes areas of overlap, shades of gradation that run north-south as well as east-west, and boundaries that have changed -- and continue to change -- through time. Recent large-scale migrations have added to the region's heterogeneity and continue to increase the degree of overlap in society, politics, and cultural terms.

Although we have also avoided the identification of national boundaries as ethnographic divisions, we do not by any means ignore the differences entailed by citizenship in the modern states of the region. Governments have extended centralized administrative institutions through land tenure registries and police, encouraged migration for a variety of purposes, and instituted national language and cultural policies. Over the past two hundred years, these new states have often ignored the ethnic contours of the hinterlands in their efforts to create national identities, and social strife in the Himalayas has often been the result. In these sections, the presentation begins with the submontane lowlands and foothills that lie below 2,500 feet, covers two mid-montane areas that fall between 2,500 and 7,500 feet, the Pahari and Tibeto-Burman, then moves to the Tibetan highlands above 7,500 feet that include the highest human settlements in the world. Part IV concludes with chapters on the two important Himalayan Valleys, Kashmir and Kathmandu.

The categories used for presenting information on each ethnographic region are consistent and provide bases for comparative cross-regional observations. They require minimal comment. "Physical Geography" depicts the distinctive landforms, climate, ecology, and communication networks. "Subsistence and Trade Patterns" describes the specific uses that humans make of their mountain environment. "Settlement Patterns" identifies the region's ethno-historical landmarks, sketches typical settlement patterns, and notes towns and religious centers of importance. "Social Relations" identifies the major ethnic group populations, cites common features in their social organization, and indicates the political processes that shaped the region. We conclude each chapter with "Cultural Continuities", a section that identifies the common and contrasting regional languages, religious traditions, and patterns of ongoing cultural evolution.

One should note that we have made no attempt to cover such vast subjects as Hinduism, Buddhism, or the histories of India or Tibet. We assume some awareness of these essential subjects that are, in many ways, pre-requisites to the study of the Himalayan region. Instead, the syllabus focuses on the particular influences these religions and civilizations exerted on the region.

In Part V, our focus is on the general themes that clarify the distinctions we have employed and address subjects that transcend regional and historical divisions. These include ethnicity and ethnic group names, Himalayan languages, indigenous spirit traditions, and modern change. Throughout the syllabus, for simplicity, we have avoided systematic diacritics for Sanskrit, Tibetan, Nepali, and the words for other languages that have been cited. For later editions, the authors welcome specific points of clarification, correction, or elaboration from those who share their special affection and concern for Himalayan peoples and their cultures.

PART ONE:

GENERAL PERSPECTIVES

Simraongarh, An Archaeologist at Work

Narayanghat Valley, Nepal

Chapter 1

THE HIMALAYAN FRONTIER

I. Introduction: Concept of Frontier

A. The Geography of Civilizations
1. Core areas or culture hearth areas where political rule, economic productivity, and culture are centered
2. Territories under central control are limited by the terrain; furthest area of control is the periphery
3. The frontier is the area beyond which the predominant systems of production in the core areas cannot be fully maintained

B. Two Types of Frontiers
1. Inner frontier -- areas circumscribed by dominant civilization, but usually separated by natural barriers (mountains, jungle, desert, etc.)
2. Boundary frontier -- areas on the far periphery of a civilization

C. Relations on the Frontier
1. In the frontier areas, two systems of production can overlap
2. Historical relationships between competing civilizations across a frontier can be cooperative or competitive; often such relationships have economic, political, and religious manifestations
3. Traders, colonizers, opportunists often compete with the core area(s) to predominate in the frontier area
4. Selective adoption of core culture traits, a common feature of local societies

II. The Himalayan Frontier (See Map 1)

A. The Himalayan region is the boundary frontier of two civilizations:
1. Indic
2. Tibetan/Chinese

B. Past and contemporary Himalayan life must be analyzed with reference to the networks extended across the region

C. Each micro-region can be analyzed according to its location and historical relations to the networks linking the two core areas (See Chapter 5)

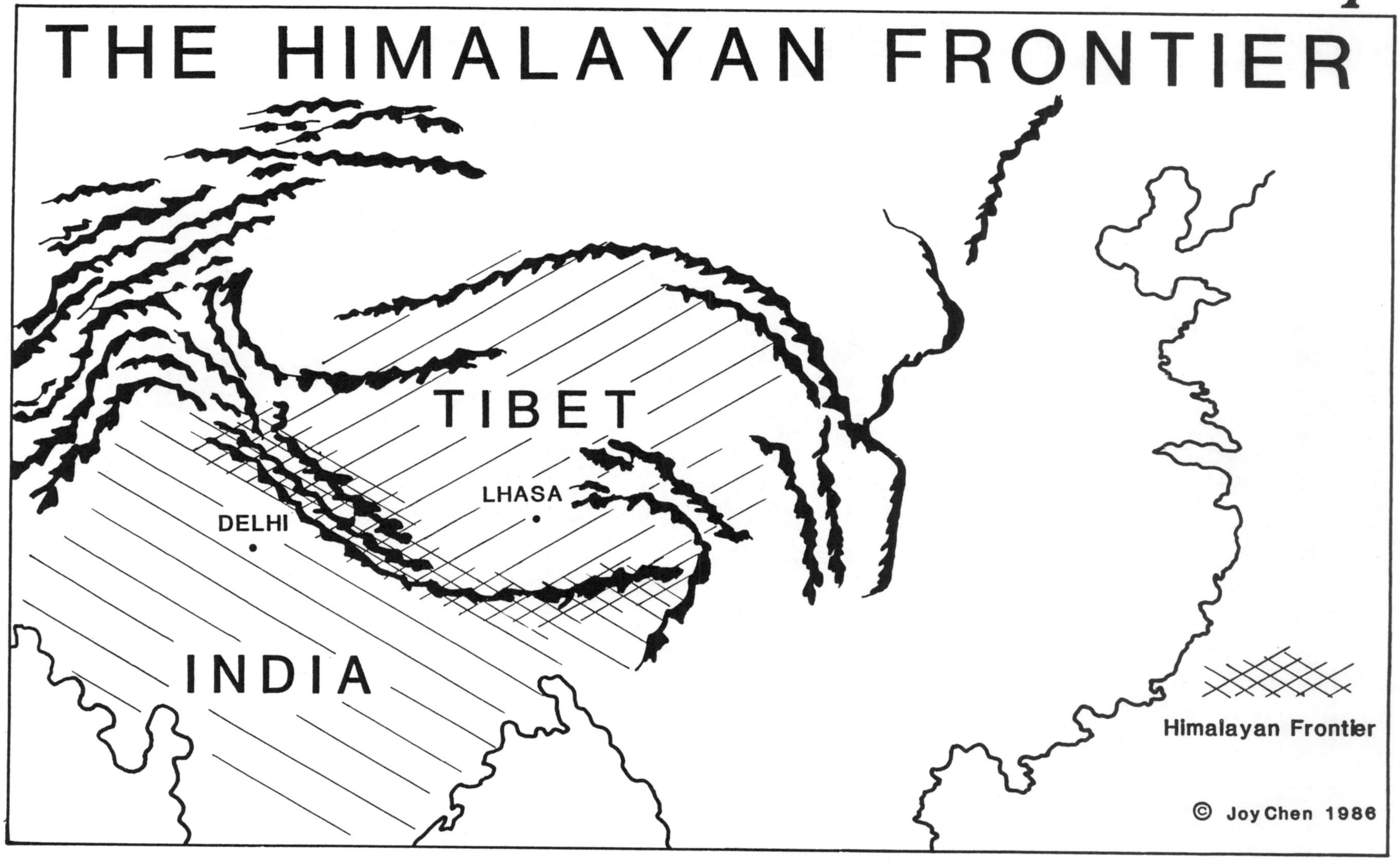

THE HIMALAYAN FRONTIER

1

TIBET

LHASA

DELHI

INDIA

Himalayan Frontier

© Joy Chen 1986

D. Pattern of colonization on the frontier: specialized groups seek out the kind of terrain and ecological niche that they had learned to exploit in their former home area

III. The Frontier of India and Indicization

A. Indicization
1. Process by which Indo-Aryan literary and political culture was imposed on non-literate peoples
2. Dominated by high caste elite, *brahmans* and *kshatriyas*
3. Introduced Indo-Aryan languages, with Sanskrit the literary, ceremonial, and inscriptional language
4. A process that began three millenia ago in core areas of Northern India, especially the upper Indus and Ganges, and affected from there, directly and indirectly, the Himalayan region, Burma, and further SE Asia
5. Spread by military force in many cases
6. Power of the "Rajput model": many ruling groups in the Himalayan region now claims Rajput origins or relations

B. Founding of Indicized kingdoms
1. Military imposition: warrior caste elite conquers an indigenous/tribal population, erects fortresses to control territory, and creates a feudal kingdom with tributary alliances with core area
   a. families branch out from nuclear settlements to colonize territory and then became the feudatories of neighbouring and/or central monarchies
   b. if the control of the latter weaken, the feudatories gradually acquire independent status
2. Indigenous chiefs adopt the civilization of the Indo-Aryans, strengthening power by adopting cultural conventions
3. Fluid shape of petty kingdoms, with changing boundaries

C. Socio-cultural Patterns and Processes
1. Local elites emulate the life-style of the greater rulers
   a. patronage of courtly literature in Sanskrit
   b. building of temples for deities of the Hindu pantheon
   c. granting of land to brahmans and other high caste groups
   d. brahmanically specified life-cycle rites (*samskaras*)
2. *Brahmans* perform key functions
   a. legitimize the *kshatriya* status of their patrons through ritual sacrifices and Vedic recitations
   b. compose *kshatriya* genealogies for those who succeeded in acquiring political power

7

       c. articulate the hierarchical order for caste society on the basis of ritual purity

       d. utilize the *dharmashastras* to compose legal codes that regulate local society

       e. restrict groups eligible to perform prestigious Hindu observances, thereby maintaining high caste boundaries and regulating claims to superior status and power

  3. Native migrants returning from the core areas contribute to the spread of Indian customs and beliefs

  4. Indicization as a vast complex of integrated socio-cultural innovations:

       a. ritual procedures (*puja*)

       b. life-cycle rites (*samskaras*)

       c. perceptions of pure and impure that regulate many aspects of interpersonal life

       d. notions of hierarchic social order based on four endogamous groups (*varna*), with any category an ideal for emulation

          1. *Brahman* (Priests)

          2. *Kshatriya* (Warriors)

          3. *Vaishya* (Artisans and Merchants)

          4. *Shudra* (Laborers)

       e. immense pantheon, with mythologies specified in Sanskrit and vernacular literatures

       f. cow veneration

       g. the north Indian calendrical system, organized around festivals (*jatras*) dedicated to important deities of the pantheon

       h. concepts of *karman* and *dharma*

D. Unevenness of the Indicization Process

  1. Some societies give up most of their traditions

  2. Many, however, still preserve the essentials of their own culture; far from being destroyed by conquerors, local elites found a framework in Indic society, transplanted and modified, within which their own society can be integrated and developed

E. Certain ecological and climactic features make some geographical regions more suitable for Indicization

  1. Regions amenable to intensive agriculture, especially rice, millet, maize, and wheat

  2. Climatic conditions where caste purity standards can be met

  3. Environments where classical Hindu cow veneration/protection complex can be implemented

F. The expansion of Indian socio-cultural influence now reaches the remotest Himalayan regions and is most recent in Arunachal Pradesh

IV. The Tibetan Frontier and Tibeticization

A. Definition: "Tibeticization"
   1. Process by which Tibetan literary and political culture was spread among non-literate peoples
   2. Dominated by high status aristocratic and monastic elite
   3. Introduced classical Tibetan as literary, ceremonial, and inscriptional language
   4. A process that began about 600 AD in central Tibet on the Tsangpo River and affected from there, directly and indirectly, areas to the northeast (Amdo, Mongolia), western China (Szechuan), the southeast (Kham), the northern Himalayan region, and central Asia
   5. Spread often by military force

B. Tibetan and Chinese relations
   1. When Chinese empires could extend the power of the imperial system to the furthest frontiers, its civilization engaged the Himalayan highlands
      a. Examples:
         1. 636: Chinese Ambassador leads an army from Tibet and Nepal to revenge abuse he suffered in north India
         2. 1415: Nepalese artistic influences in China
         3. 1792: Chinese-Gurkha war brought the Chinese army into Tibet and Nepal
         4. 1959: direct Chinese rule over Tibet
         5. 1962: war between India and China across the northern border
         6. 1986: Chinese negotiate with India on borders of Arunachal Pradesh
   2. Tibetan political power, centered in Lhasa, oscillated from almost total independence to absorption within the Chinese empire

C. Socio-cultural Patterns and Processes:
   1. Submission to monastic landlords and conversion to Tibetan Buddhism
      a. stories among many of the frontier peoples -- Tamangs, Magars, Gurung -- contain origin myths relating them to central Tibet
      b. the Lepchas retain a tradition of Tibetan lamas destroying all evidence of their indigenous culture upon their subjugation and conversion

9

2. Pattern of monastic/nobility alliance: a ruler's brother or uncle appointed as chief abbot of the polity's most important monastery, guaranteeing the landowning classes' solidarity
3. Institutional networks of the main monastic schools dominate the formation of Tibetanized polities and link periphery regions to the center
    a. young initiates go to larger, more central monasteries for training
    b. great lamas travel to the peripheral regions to preach and heal
    c. different schools from the central area extend their monasteries across Tibet and compete for territory and patronage
    d. *Jisa* mechanism of monastery finance encourages monk-treasurers to set up subscriptions
        1. laymen pay for the performance of rituals
        2. monks free to accumulate excess funds and use them to establish new satellite monasteries, make pilgrimages to new areas
4. The extension of political control across the landscape often correlates with the networks of caravan trade

D. Lamas perform key functions
1. Provide prestigious Buddhist "pedigrees" to allied rulers
2. Supply the cultural agenda to guarantee prosperity, display piety, and perpetuate noble rule

E. In religious terms, the Tibeticization of a settled area is described as the conversion of indigenous mountain gods to Buddhism by a great saint or deity

F. Comparisons with Indicization
1. Far fewer people in the core areas of Tibet
2. The inner frontiers separating settlements more vast
3. The extent of socio-cultural transition on the far Tibetan frontiers much less thoroughgoing
4. Later beginnings of the process in Tibet (7th Century)
5. Indian origins of many facets of Tibetan culture and Indian influences on China often make it difficult to characterize some traits as either Indian or Tibetan
6. In both societies, ranked endogamous groups define social organization hierarchies

V. Islamization

    A. Predominant in the Northwest region, especially in modern Pakistan and Kashmir; also important in some submontane areas

    B. Central role of the ulama in defining Islamic orthodoxy, maintaining mosques, and education

VI. SUMMARY: HIMALAYAS AS INDO-TIBETAN FRONTIER

    A. Historical Dialectic: Indic and Tibetan civilizations interact throughout Himalayan history over the past millenium and a half

    B. Indian and Chinese civilizations have interacted in Tibet throughout history; in the Himalayas, Indian influences predominate in some areas, but Tibetan influences are dominant in many others

    C. When assessing the ethno-history of any part of the Himalayan region, the macro-regional dynamics must be balanced with the regional and micro-regional frontier variables.

INDICIZED POLITIES	TIBETICIZED POLITIES
center-periphery relations more direct	networks looser, in more severe terrain
culture hearth of North Indian plains; one of most densely settled areas in the world	culture hearth of central Tibetan plateau; one of the most sparsely settled areas in the world
rice-cow subsistence system with settlements clustered where irrigation and rice cultivation irrigation and rice cultivation are ideal	cold crop, herding subsistence with settlements clustered where water, soil, climate allow fixed agriculture
dominated by kshatriya-brahman alliances	dominated by nobility-monastic alliances
high caste landlord elite	nobility and monastic landlord elite
expansive patrilineage dynamic	less expansive system
caste hierarchy as socio-religious ideal	endogamous social groupings and monastic religious ideal
Indic calendar	Chinese calendar

Figure 1: Socio-Cultural Comparisons on the Indo-Tibetan Frontier

Recommended Readings and References

Aris, Michael. "The Tibetan Borderlands," in Michael Aris ed. *Lamas, Princes, and Brigands: Joseph Rock's Photographs of the Tibetan Borderlands of China*. New York: China House Gallery, 1992, 13-18.

Berreman, Gerald D. "Cultures and Peoples of the Himalayas," *Asian Survey* 3, 1963: 289-304.

Embree, Ainslie. "Frontiers into Boundaries: From the Traditional to the Modern State," in Richard Fox ed. *Realm and Region in Traditional India*. Durham: Duke University Press, 1977, 255-280.

Jones, Rex L. "Sanskritization in Eastern Nepal," *Ethnology* 15 (1), 1976, 63-75.

Lamb, Alstair. *Asian Frontiers: Studies of a Continuing Problem*. London: Pall Mall Press, 1968.

Lattimore, Owen. "The Frontier in History," in Own Lattimore ed. *Studies in Frontier History: Collected Papers 1928-1958*. Paris: Mouton, 1962, 469-491.

Leach, Edmund. "Frontiers of `Burma'," *Comparative Studies in Society and History* III, 1960-1, 49-68.

Lewis, Todd T. "Himalayan Frontier Trade: Newar Diaspora Merchants and Buddhism," in Martin Brauen ed. *Anthropology of Tibet and the Himalayas*. Zurich: Volkerkundemuseum, 1993, 165-178.

Miller, Beatrice D. "The Web of Tibetan Monasticism," *Journal of Asian Studies* XX (2), 1960, 197-204.

Miller, Robert J. "The Buddhist Monastic Economy: The Jisa Mechanism," *Comparative Studies in Society and History* IV, 1962, 427-438.

Prescott, J.R.V. *The Geography of Frontiers and Boundaries*. NY: Basic Books, 1965.

Rocher, Ludo. "The Concept of Boundaries in Classical India," in Peter Gaeffke and David Utz eds. *The Countries of South Asia: Boundaries, Extensions, and Interrelations*. Philadelphia: University of Pennsylvania Press, 1988, 3-11.

Samuel, Geoffrey. "Tibet and Southeast Asian Highlands: Rethinking the Intellectual Context of Tibetan Studies," in Per Kvaerne ed. *Tibetan Studies, II.* Oslo: Institute for Comparative Research in Human Culture, 1994, 696-710.

Schwartzberg, Joseph. "Cartography of Greater Tibet and Mongolia," in Woodward Harley ed. *The History of Cartography, Volume 2 (Book 2).* Chicago: University of Chicago Press, 1994, 607-681.

Highland Settlement

13

Mid-Montane Watershed South of Pokhara

Chapter 2

THE MOUNTAINS AND SUBSISTENCE

I. Introduction to the Geography of the Himalayas (Maps 2,3, & 4)

   A. Young mountain range (25 million years old) that is still rising; all flora and fauna from neighboring regions, with almost no specially evolved species native to the range

   B. Region a natural marvel: tropical heat and arctic cold occur within 50 miles, creating a rich variety of life unique on the earth

   C. Regional climate: in general, eastern areas wetter than western areas

   D. Regular vertical zonation patterns
      1. Mean temperature drops 11 degrees Fahrenheit for every 3,400 feet increase in altitude
      2. Treeline
         a. coincides with elevation levels having mean temperature of 50 degrees Fahrenheit or more on the warmest days of the year
         b. higher on southern exposures than northern

   E. Ecologic Zones (Map 3)
      1. Aeolian
         a. tree line and above
         b. exposed rock and ice-snow covered forms
         c. life limited to bacteria, fungi, insects, crustaceans that subsist on airborne nutrients
         d. severest climate
      2. Alpine (13,500-snowline)
         a. treeline to snowline
         b. harsh winters, short summers
         c. shallow soils with scrub trees, sedge and grass meadows, wildflowers
         d. low moisture
      3. Subalpine (12,000 ft-alpine)
         a. transition zone between alpine and temperate zones
         b. stunted trees, especially fir, birch, pine

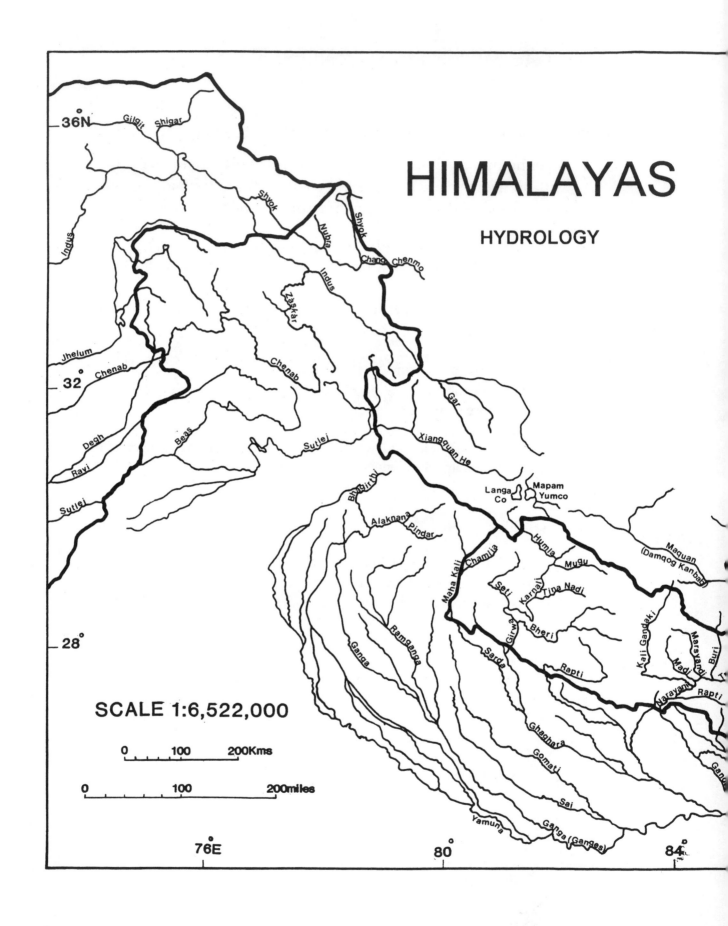

HIMALAYAS

HYDROLOGY

SCALE 1:6,522,000

0   100   200Kms

0   100   200miles

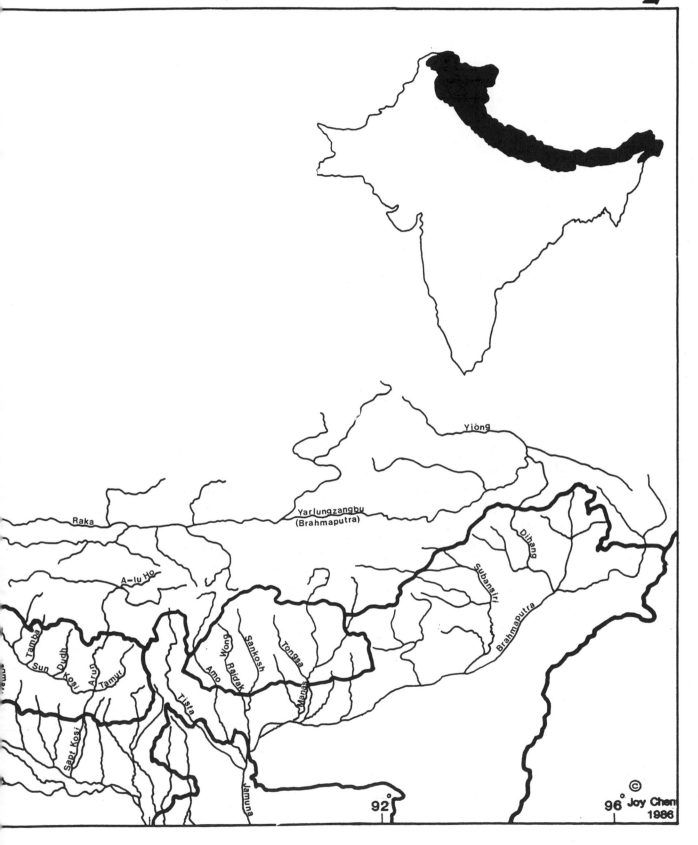

Raka

Yarlungzangbu
(Brahmaputra)

Yiòng

A-lu Ho

Dihang

Subansiri

Brahmaputra

Tamba

Sun

Dudh

Kosi

Arun

Tamur

Tista

Amo

Wong

Raidak

Sankosh

Tongsa

Manas

Sapt Kosi

Jamuna

92°

96° Joy Chen
1986

2

4. Temperate (3,000 ft-subalpine)
    a. rich forest occurs naturally in this region, conifers at higher elevations, hardwoods lower
    b. rhododendron and bamboo common in central and eastern regions
    c. most distinctly Himalayan fauna found in this region
5. Tropical/Subtropical
    a. plains flora and fauna
    b. sal tree, large pine stands common

III. Geographical and Climatic Characteristics of the Ethnographic Regions (Maps 4 and 6)

A. The Submontane Region
    1. Land below 2,500 feet, from Himachal Pradesh (HP) to Arunachal Pradesh (AP)
    2. Landforms
        a. outer Terai, babar: low foothills
        b. inner Terai, duns: small valleys
        c. volatile rivers that change course
    3. Vast tropical forests increasingly cleared for settlement after the eradication of malaria
    4. Very hot summer season; land often inundated during the monsoon
    5. Brahmaputra Valley a distinct sub-region

B. The Mid-montane Region
    1. Land from 2,500 - 7,500 ft., from Kashmir to Arunachal Pradesh
    2. Landforms
        a. Mahabharat Lekh mountain range and subsidiary ridges from the high Himalayas
        b. major rivers that have their headwaters on the north side of the high Himalayas and cut through the entire region
    3. Mixed hardwood forests, with large tracts of rhododendron, bamboo
    4. Temperate climate, with wide microclimactic variations
    5. Most areas inhabitable all year
    6. Large valleys that have supported expansive centers of civilization
        a. Kashmir Valley
        b. Kathmandu Valley

C. Highlands Region
    1. Lands above 7,500 ft. on both sides of the high Himalayan peaks
    2. Landforms
        a. inhabitable areas across the highest mountain range on earth
        b. upland plateaus and valleys
        c. shaped by major rivers, glaciation, and avalanches

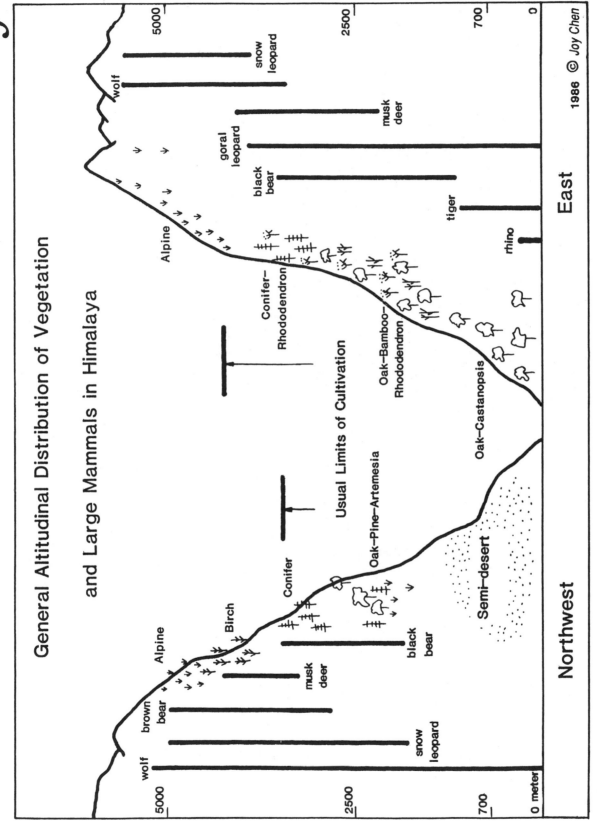

General Altitudinal Distribution of Vegetation
and Large Mammals in Himalaya

1986 © Joy Chen

3

3. Hardwood and evergreen forests give way to scrub species by 14,000 ft., with only specially adapted ground plants above
4. Cold climate, with short growing season and severe winter conditions

IV. Effects of Mountain Topography on Himalayan Societies

A. Terrain creates social isolation and minimizes contact with neighboring regions

B. Venue of refuge: recurring tradition of vanquished plains and Tibetan plateau nobility escaping to the mountains where many establish new kingdoms

C. Preservation of ancient cultural traits
   1. Many of the traditions of India and Tibet were transplanted to the hills
   2. Isolation and freedom from direct rule enabled peoples in the region to retain traditions that were later lost in the core areas
   3. From ancient times, the remoteness and isolation of region have drawn pilgrims and religious aspirants
      a. communities established by religious leaders often became important towns
      b. main types:
         1. Hindu *ashrams*
         2. Buddhist monasteries

D. Isolation and inaccessibility responsible for slow penetration of technology
   1. Agricultural crops:
      a. corn in 1600s
      b. potatoes introduced in 1840's
      c. current spread of new strains
   2. Mechanization
      a. transportation
      b. electrification
   3. Modern medicine

V. General Subsistence Factors

A. Mountain climate and terain support fragile ecosystems

B. Key elements in human adaptation: local rainfall, water resources, soil quality, altitude, winds

C. Subsistence often depends on precise adaptation to the local environment with little margin

VI. Subsistence Patterns

A. Hunting and Gathering
  1. Reliance on hunting, fishing, and gathering wild foods
  2. Supports low population densities
  3. Once common across the inner-frontiers and dense forestlands; now only a few scattered hunting and gathering tribes remain, mostly in Arunachal Pradesh

B. Nomadic Pastoralism
  1. Living itinerantly with herds of animals that provide a small community's subsistence
  2. Supports very low population densities
  3. Only a few groups remain in the region
      a. Gujars of Kashmir, Himachal Pradesh, Uttar Pradesh
      b. Scattered Gaddi pastoralists of Himachal Pradesh
      c. Ahirs in the Assam Valley and Terai
      d. Tibetan and other highlanders

C. Slash and Burn Agriculture (*Jhum*)
  1. Cycle: cutting down vegetation on a new site, burning it, planting crops with bamboo poles on the land fertilized by the ash, then moving on after several years
  2. Common where land was plentiful and labor force limited
  3. Only practiced today in remote areas, due to state laws banning the practice

D. Subsistence Farming
  1. Capable of supporting large populations on suitable lands
  2. Most inhabitants are subsistence farmers
  3. Most households rely on complex mixtures of grain production, animal husbandry, and trade
  4. Himalayan peasants among the most isolated in the world
  5. Food crops:
      a. distribution: (example study in central Nepal) maize 39%, rice 33%, potatoes 14%, millet 8%, wheat 5%, barley 1%
      b. systems of inter-cropping have been highly developed
      c. usual division between irrigated lands (Nep. *khet*) and dry fields that depend on rainfall (Nep. *bari*)

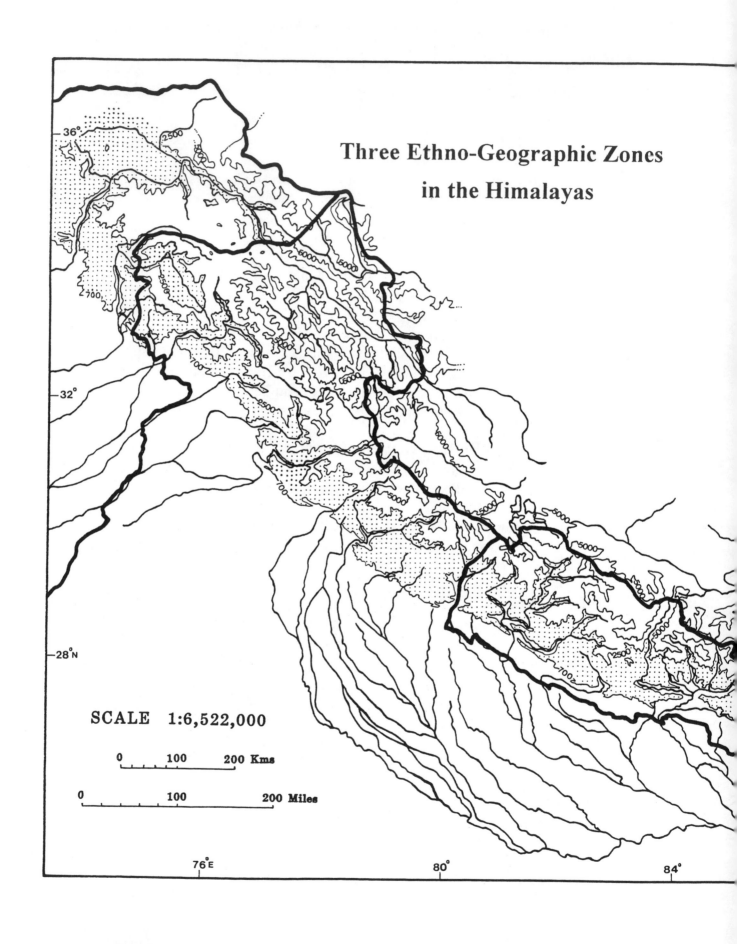

Three Ethno-Geographic Zones
in the Himalayas

SCALE 1:6,522,000

0   100   200 Kms

0   100   200 Miles

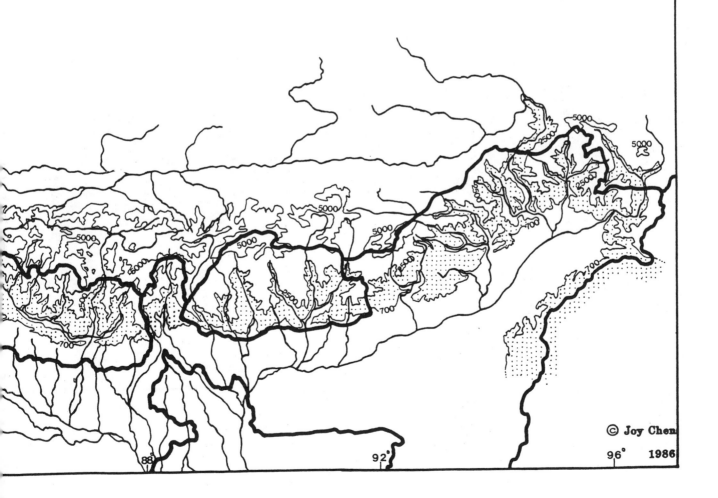

4

feet   meters

16,404 ———— 5000 limit of settlements

                 highlands

8202 ———— 2500

                 midmontane

2297 ———— 700

                 submontane

5000

5000

5000

5000

5000

5000

700

700

700

700

88°

92°

96°

© Joy Chen

1986

6. Common cash crops:
   a. medicinal plants
   b. citrus
   c. ginger
   d. turmeric
   e. hashish
   f. cotton
   g. cardamom
   h. jute
   i. tea
7. Many hill agriculturalists do not produce enough to fulfill their household needs
8. Common form of village cooperation at peak agricultural seasons: households form groups that work each others' fields by rotation
9. Twice-daily meal among prosperous households: *dal-bhat tarkari*, "lentil-rice-vegetables", spiced with chili peppers
10. Typical residence pattern: with small landholders, there are few advantages for sons to manage the estate jointly; once married, they establish separate households on inherited land parcels

Preparing the *khet*, Eastern Nepal

Recommended Readings and References

Bishop, Barry C. "The Changing Geoecology of Karnali Zone, Western Nepal Himalaya: A Case of Stress," *Arctic and Alpine Research 10* (2), 1978, 531-543.

Blair, Katherine D. *Four Villages*: *Architecture in Nepal*. Los Angeles: Craft and Folk Art Museum, 1983.

Cronin, Edward W. Jr. *The Arun: A Natural History of the World's Deepest Valley*. Boston: Houghton Mifflin, 1979.

Fricke, Thomas. "Introduction: Human Ecology in the Himalaya," *Human Ecology 17* (2), 1989, 131-145. (Other articles from this issue focus on the Himalayan region.)

Goldstein, Melvyn C. and Donald Messerschmidt. "The Significance of Latitudinality in Himalayan Mountain Ecosystems," *Human Ecology 8* (2), 1980, 117-134.

Guillet, David. "Toward a Cultural Ecology of Mountains: The Central Andes and Himalayas Compared," *Current Anthropology* 24 (5), 1983, 561-574.

Hoffpauir, Robert. "Subsistence Strategy and Its Ecological Consequences in the Nepal Himalaya," *Anthropos* 73, 1978, 215-252.

Jhingran, A.G. "Geology of the Himalaya," in J.S. Lall ed. *The Himalaya: Aspects of Change*. Delhi: Oxford University Press, 1981, 77-98.

Mani, Anna. "The Climate of the Himalaya," in J.S. Lall ed. *The Himalaya: Aspects of Change*. Delhi: Oxford University Press, 1981, Chapter 1.

Molnar, P. and Tapponnier, P. "The Collision between India and Eurasia," *Scientific American* 5 (1), 1977, 30-41.

Pant, S.D. *The Social Economy of the Himalayans*. London: Allen and Unwin, 1935.

Stainton, J.D.A. *Forests of Nepal*. New York: Hanfer Publishing Company, 1972.

Uhlig, Harald. "Rice Cultivation in the Himalayas," *German Scholars in India II*, 1976, 296-326.

Trading Caravan, Western Nepal

Chapter 3

TRADE AND ECONOMIC NETWORKS

I. Introduction (See Map 5)

A. As states have extended their domain across the "inner frontiers" of the region, artisans and merchants have traveled to pursue their livelihoods

B. Major towns in the Himalayan region developed at trade centers on regional and all-Asian trade routes

C. Succession of Communication Networks
   1. Old foot and pony trails
   2. Railroad lines
   3. Automobile-truck routes
   4. Airplane landing strips

D. Seasonality determines movement:
   1. Most highland passess are only open during limited periods
   2. Mid-montane travel precarious during the peak monsoon rains
   3. Submontane region is best crossed during the winter season

II. Trade and Economics

A. Types of Trade
   1. Long distance caravan trade that specialized in luxury goods moving between Tibet and India almost completely stopped after 1959
      a. from Tibetan side: brick tea, tobacco, sheepskins, furs, dried meat, wool cloth, carpets, clothes, Chinese silks, silver ornaments, porcelain cups, ritual objects, hand-printed books
      b. from Nepal: dyes, ghee, dried potatoes, unrefined sugar, incense, hand-made paper, buffalo hides, cotton cloth
   2. The wool/salt↔grain networks resumed in 1970s after being disrupted following the Chinese takeover of Tibet in 1959; presence of Indian salt has diminished the former profitability of the trade
   3. Petty traders set up shops to export local surpluses and to import items for sale in small settlements

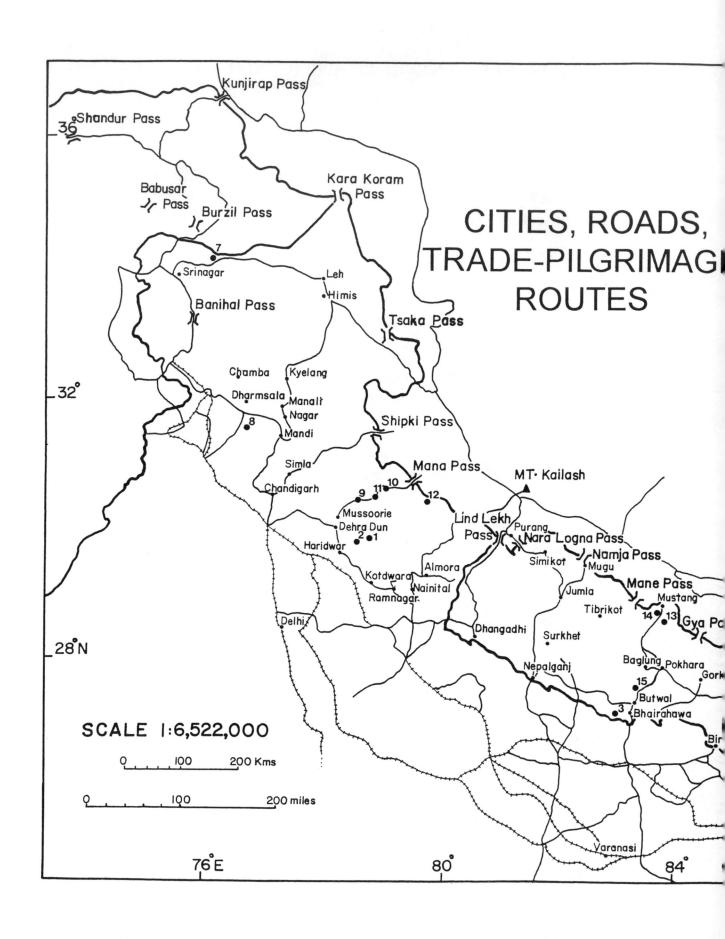

CITIES, ROADS,
TRADE-PILGRIMAG
ROUTES

Kunjirap Pass

Shandur Pass

36

Kara Koram
Pass

Babusar
Pass
Burzil Pass

7

Srinagar

Leh

Himis

Banihal Pass

Tsaka Pass

Chamba
Kyelang

Dharmsala

Manali

8
Nagar

Mandi

Shipki Pass

Simla

Mana Pass

MT· Kailash

Chandigarh

9 11 10

12

Mussoorie

Dehra Dun

Lind Lekh
Pass
Purang

Nara Logna Pass

Haridwar

2 1

Namja Pass

Almora

Simikot

Mugu

Kotdwara

Nainital

Jumla

Mane Pass

Ramnagar

Mustang

Tibrikot

14 13 Gya Pa

Delhi

Dhangadhi

Surkhet

Baglung Pokhara

28°N

Nepalganj

Gork

15

Butwal

SCALE 1:6,522,000

3 Bhairahawa

0   100   200 Kms

Bir

0   100   200 miles

32°

Varanasi

76°E

80°

84°

5

.	City	6	Sibsagar
⏝	Pass	7	Amarnath
▬	Country Boundary	8	Jwalamukti
—	Road, Route	9	Uttarkashi
+++	Railroad	10	Gangotri
●	Pilgrimage Place	11	Kedarnath
1	Devaprayag	12	Badrinath
2	Rishikesh	13	Muktinath
3	Lumbini	14	Salagrama
4	Janakpur	15	Ridi
5	Hajo	16	Pasupatinath

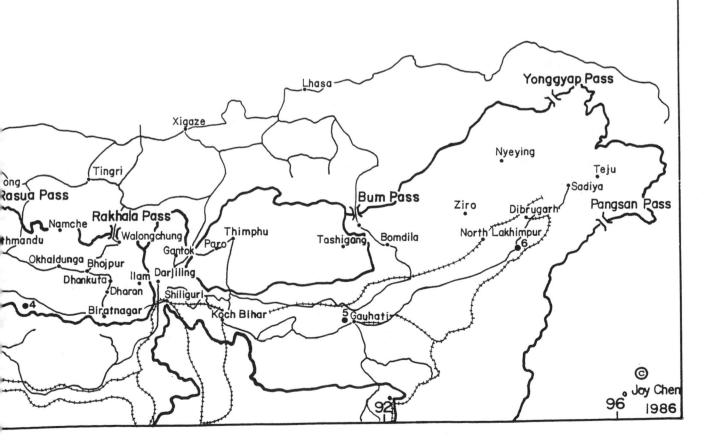

4. Modern business and trading group: the Marwaris
   a. a class of Indian merchants originally from Rajasthan established trans-India networks that include the Himalayas
   b. specialize in essential commodities: salt, grains, cloth, cooking oil, kerosene
5. Trade among pastoralists involving long nomadic cycles (up to 10 months) in which individuals trade for profitable commodities they transport to other places
   a. conducted at yearly fairs where agriculturalists and pastoralists meet
   b. may combine many of the elements above
   c. examples: highlanders of Ladakh, Humla, D'ing-ri
6. People maintaining shops and hotels for travelers

B. Trading families often maintain ethnic alliances along trade routes; in places, these groups have close alliances with ruling powers

C. Systems of ritual friendship (*mit*) are common among almost every ethnic group; these relationships often solidify trade arrangements across ethnic boundaries

D. Common presence of rotating credit associations (Nep. *dhikurs*; New. *guthi*)
   1. Households join together and contribute equally to form a common fund
   2. Each household gains access to the capital fund by yearly rotation and must repay the principal with interest at the end of the term

E. In many areas, trade is an essential part of the household's survival strategy

F. In Nepal, the weekly or monthly *hat bazaar*:
   1. Markets held in the same place, often with government sponsorship (and, if so, taxation)
   2. Surplus crops sold
   3. Animals sold: cattle, buffalo, yak, sheep, goats, horses
   4. Animal products: wool, ghee, meat
   5. Consumer goods for sale: cloth, taxes, school supplies, salt, spices, tea, sugar, tobacco
   6. Petty entrepreneurs from villages attend *hat bazaars* to buy goods for resale in the home area

Porters at a Teahouse, Eastern Nepal

At the *Hat Bazaar*, Bhojpur

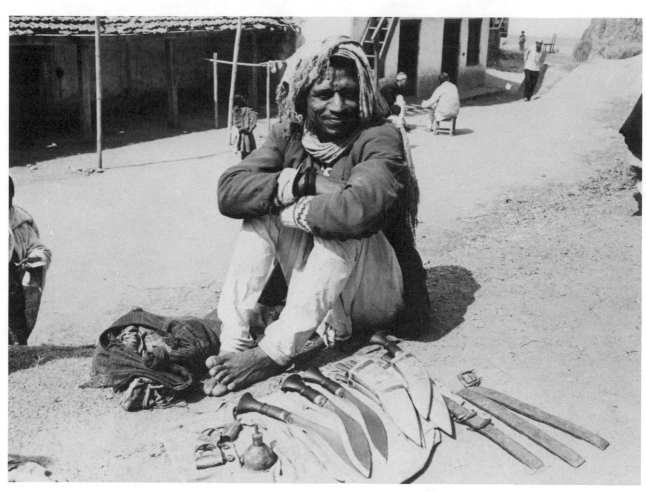

Itinerant *Khukuri* Craftsman, Central Nepal

G. Artisans
   1. Travel in regular cycles across the hills to offer their services at hat bazaars and in villages
   2. Work for specific clients done on a cash or barter basis
   3. Examples:
       a. tailors
       b. potters
       c. metal workers, especially blacksmiths
       d. wood workers
       e. Muslim cloth carders

H. Moneylenders
   1. Prominent large landowners and shopkeepers with excess cash and/or capital grant loans to individuals, most commonly when agricultural crops are planted but not yet harvested or when a marriage entails high costs
   2. Cycle of exploitation:
       a. excessive interest rates lead to failure to repay loans on time, incurring further indebtedness
       b. debtor becomes a dependent client of the lender, is obliged to support him in special circumstances; in political arena, especially in elections, these relationships are especially important
       c. if possible, lender forces debtor to mortgage his lands and acquires them in the case of default
   3. Moneylenders are chief figures in the local economies
       a. Bahun-Chetris in east Nepal
       b. Thakali shopkeepers in central Nepal
       c. Newars along prominent trade routes, especially those linked to Kathmandu

III. Pilgrimage Networks

A. Trade and pilgrimage overlap part of world pattern: close linkage between religion and trade, pilgrims and merchants, the great temple and the bazaar, the ritual supply stall and the pilgrimage destination

B. Both networks are the major pathways that cross the Himalayan region and are fundamental to the diffusion of change in the mountains

C. Ancient history of Himalayan pilgrimage evident in early Hindu textual references

D. Sites throughout the Himalayas known for special spiritual forces and regarded as venues for pilgrimage by both Indians and Tibetans (See Chapter 5)

E. Pilgrimage sites extend into the furthest frontier areas not settled by those in the core areas
   1. Important Indian sites are in the highlands
   2. Notable Tibetan sites in the mid-montane and submontane zones

F. Important shrines across the region hold a religious fair (*mela*) once a year, and pilgrims time their travels to be there at these times; merchants also travel to offer food and wares, making them both religious and commercial events

G. Restaurant and hotel business networks form around pilgrimage routes so that pilgrimage and trade networks converge

H. Pilgrims introduce influences from their home regions, regularly linking sites in the Himalayas to their respective civilization centers

Recommended Readings and References

Bhardwaj, Surinder Mohan. *Hindu Places of Pilgrimage in India*. Berkeley: University of California Press, 1973.

Curtin, Philip D. *Cross-Cultural Trade in World History*. Cambridge University Press, 1984.

Fisher, James F. *Trans-Himalayan Traders*. Berkeley: University of California Press, 1986.

Fürer-Haimendorf, Christoph von. *Himalayan Traders*. New York: St. Martins, 1975.

Lewis, Todd T. and Shakya, Daya Ratna. "Contributions to the History of Nepal: Eastern Newar Diaspora Settlements," *Contributions to Nepalese Studies* 15, 1988, 26-65.

Messerschmidt, Donald. "Gateway-Hinter Relations in Changing Nepal," *Contributions to Nepalese Studies* 8, 1980, 21-40.

Mikesell, Steven and Shrestha, J. "Mercantilism and Domestic Industry in West-Central Nepal: Significance for the Anthropological Study of the Community," *Occasional Papers in Sociology and Anthropology* 2, 1990, 77-89.

Indian Pilgrims near Muktinath

Bauddha Stupa, Kathmandu Valley

Chapter 4

THE STRUCTURE OF HIMALAYAN REGIONS AND MICRO-REGIONS

I. Settlement Patterns

    A. Sites develop in places close to crucial resources or geographic features
- 1. Broad valleys suitable for irrigation and intensive grain cultivation
- 2. Control points for Himalayan trade
- 3. Access to mineral resources
- 4. Strategic military positions
- 5. Pilgrimage sites

    B. Sites possessing many of these characteristics support the highest population densities

II. Central Places

    A. Centers of production:
- 1. Metalwork
- 2. Weaving
- 3. Mining
- 4. Crafts manufacturing
- 5. Industry
- 6. Other

    B. Elites in central places dominate exchange relations with hinterland regions

III. Gateway Communities

    A. Trade entrepots and trans-shipment points

    B. Resting stops for caravans, especially points leading to passes and bridges that concentrate traffic

IV. "Galactic Polities"

A. A recurring form of political articulation in empires, kingdoms, and outlying settlements

B. Evolved in regions when dominant centers established allied settlements into a tributary state system

C. These networks are maintained by political relations, kinship exchanges, migration, trade, religious influences, and cultural movements

D. Over time, changes occur in the system: former secondary centers rise to prominence and dominant centers fall

E. As technological advances modify the movement through the hills, especially with the building of new roads and the availablility of vehicles that speed transit, the character of the polities and sub-polities is transformed in demography, trade, language, religion

V. Complementarity of Trade and Pilgrimage:

A. Traders profit from the development of pilgrimage routes and the patronage of temples

B. Pilgrims profited from the routes that provide safe travel and minimal services

C. Pattern of local residents entering the network as traders and middlemen
   1. Using their center to their own advantage, they set up "trade diasporas" that place their allies -- usually kin -- throughout the network
   2. Often one ethnic group comes to dominate movement in a single network
      a. connections along the trail give advantages that made the group more competitive
      b. examples: Newars, Thakalis, Sherpas, Marwaris

Recommended Readings and References

Barth, Frederik. "Ecological Relationships of Ethnic Groups in Swat, North Pakistan,"
American Anthropologist 58, 1956, 1083-1089.

Messerschmidt, Donald A. "Gateway-Hinter Relations in Changing Nepal,"
Contributions to Nepalese Studies, 8, 1980, 21-40.

Tambiah, Stanley J. "The Galactic Polity: The Structure of Traditional Kingdoms in
Southeast Asia," *Annals of the New York Academy of Sciences* 293, 1977, 69-97.

Sadhu in the Market, Kathmandu

Himalayan Scene from a Drepung Monastery Mural, Lhasa

Chapter 5

THE HIMALAYAS IN INDIAN AND TIBETAN TRADITIONS

I. The Indian Tradition

    A. Sanskrit terms

        1. *HIMA* + *ALAYA* = "snow" + "abode"

        2. *Himavat*, a synonym

    B. Himalayan kinship in Indian myth:

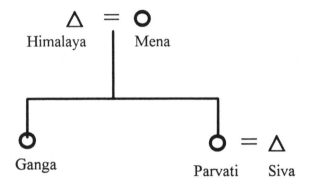

    C. Mentioned in Vedic Texts

        1. One of the frontier regions of "*Bharata*", classical name for India

        2. Cited as a source of medicinal herbs in Atharva Veda

    D. Himalayas in early Indian geographical thinking:

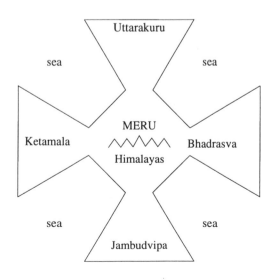

E. Indian Medicine:
    1. Gupta references to shaman-doctors from the region who bring special
       herbs
    2. Shiva identified as "Lord of *Vaidyas*" and his home in the Himalayas
       associated with the many medicinal herbs found there

F. Himalayas as places of revelation
    1. Vedic tradition: Vyasa taught Vedas to disciples there
    2. According to some schools, the Himalayan peaks are the dwelling place
       of the deities; region referred to as *devalaya*
    3. Many Gods of the pantheon have mountain abodes:
        a. Shiva, Parvati -- Mt. Kailash
        b. Annapurna Devi -- Annapurna
        c. Ganesh -- Ganesh Himal
        d. Vishnu -- Gosainkund
        e. Hanuman -- Bandarpunch (UP)
    4. Himalayas as place where *vidyadharas* ("spirits") live.

G. Himalayas as pilgrimage destination:
    1. *Darshana* ("sighting") of mountains highly praised; a notable passage
       from the *Skanda Purana* states: "In a hundred years of the gods, I could
       not tell thee of the glories of the Himalayas; As dew is dried by the
       morning sun, so are the sins of mankind by the sight of the Himalayas."
    2. The *Mahabharata* refers to religious suicide by the aged on pilgrimage
       to the region
    3. Ancient history of Himalayan pilgrimage as seen in early Hindu textual
       references
        a. *Mahabharata* (200 AD) mentions:
            1. Baramula, Kashmir
            2. Jwalamukhi
            3. Yamunotri
            4. Gangotri
            5. Kailash-Manasarovar
            6. Gandaki source: Salagrama (Nepal)
            7. Gaurisikhara (Nepal)
            8. Kirtika: the Arun, Sunkosi, Tamur confluence (Nepal)
        b. *Matsya Purana* (1200 AD) mentions:
            1. Baramula, Kashmir
            2. Varahisaila, Kashmir
            3. Acchoda, Kashmir
            4. Jwalamukhi
            5. Kedara
            6. Badritirtha
            7. Manasarovar

8. Salagrama
9. Gaurisikhara
10. Pashupati
4. Modern pilgrimage sites:
   a. Amarnath
   b. Gangotri
   c. Jwalamukhi
   d. Kedarnath
   e. Badrinath
   f. Lake Manasarowar
   g. Kailash
   h. Hardwar
   i. Rishikesh
   j. Muktinath
   k. Pashupati
   l. Kamakhya

H. Himalayas as places for retreat and refuge
1. Pandhava brothers at end of the *Mahabharata* retire there
2. Folklore of many Himalayan peoples recounts their reputed Rajput ancestors leaving the plains for settlement in the mountains

I. Region important for the *Natha* cult
1. Associated with the ninth century *Kanphata* yogins Gorakhnath and Matsyendranath who travel throughout Assam and other Himalayan regions to meditate and preach
2. Commonplace "*nath*" ending to place names in the region reflects this influence
3. Chief monasteries of present sect are in Gorakhpur and in Savarikot, Nepal

J. Buddhist Traditions
1. A refrain in Buddhist texts is to Shakyamuni Buddha, "the sage born on the slopes of the Himalayas"
2. A Tibetan text notes the first "18 Schools of Buddhism"; five of these are *Mahasanghikas*; of these, one is called the "Himavat School"
3. Later Chinese textual traditions identify "16 *Sthaviras*" who protect the *Dharma*; two are from the region:
   a. Abhedya ("Himalaya")
   b. Kanakavatsa ("Kashmir")
4. In the Pali texts, Lake Manasarovar is called "Anotatta" and said to be protected by the *Naga* Pannaka; *Visuddhimagga* lists 7 lakes in the Himalayas:
   a. Sihapapata
   b. Hamsapatana

   c. Kannamundaka
   d. Rathakara
   e. Anotatta
   f. Chaddanta
   g. Kunala
  5. Buddhaghosa mentions the Himalayan abode of the *karavika* bird, whose marvelous singing causes all animals to stop in rapt wonderment; singing is compared to the voice of the Buddha
  6. Tibetan text asserts that Asita, the sage who visits the Buddha at birth and predicts his destiny, "comes from the Himalayas"

K. As frontier, place of "conversion" of tribal peoples and contestation between Hinduism and Buddhism

II. The Tibetan Tradition

A. Buddhist

  1. Mountains compared to Buddhist *chorten* (*stupas*)
  2. Himalayas as an area converted by the *bodhisattva* Avalokiteshvara
  3. Mt. Kailash (Tib. Ti-se) as locale where Padmasambhava defeated Bon priests
  4. Lake Manasarovar ruled over by two *nagas*, Nanda and Upananda
  5. Kathmandu Valley sites of Buddhist hierophany:
   a. Svayambhu
   b. Bauddha
  6. Many pilgrimage spots in the Himalayas associated with Padmasambhava, Milarepa, and other saints
  7. Tradition of twenty-four Chakrasamvara sites in India, two in the Himalayan region:
   a. Kulu
   b. Hajo-Kamakhya, Assam
  8. Tradition of Kushinagara, the place of the Buddha's decease, being in Assam at Hajo
  9. Places where "hidden valleys" (Tib. *khembalung*) are thought to exist
   a. Sages dwell in some, where climate is mild and where an ideal Buddhist society exists
   b. Myth of Shambala: hidden valley where a divine Buddhist saint-king will arise to lead in the restoration of Buddhism
  10. Region where tantric objects (Tib. *gter-ma*) were hidden by past sages for the benefit of future generations; in the words of one text:
"For each important valley there is an important hidden treasure: these are signs of Padmasambhava; for each little place there is a minor hidden treasure: these are also signs of Padmasambhava."
(Quoted from the *gter-lun* of Ratna-glin-pa)

B. Mount Kailash in the Bon tradition
   1. Ancient ruler of Zhang-zhung kingdom identified as coming from this region
   2. 360 Ge-khod, emanations of the terrifying nine-headed deity "Angry God", thought to reside on this peak

III. Other Traditional Sources

A. Mongolian Tradition: Folk God "White Old Man" lives in the "Snowy White mountains to the far southwest," i.e. the Himalayas

B. Early Chinese imperial records are aware of the Himalayas, and the writings by Chinese pilgrims on their travels to India brought the region into popular Chinese awareness

C. Myth of "Gold Digging Ants" located in the Indus region found in early Greek histories and later highland folklore

D. Burmese forest monk stories refer to the region as an important pilgrimage area

The Mongolian "White Old Man"

Recommended Readings and References

Bhardwaj, Surinder Mohan. *Hindu Places of Pilgrimage in India.* Berkeley: University of California Press, 1973.

Bernbaum, Edwin. *The Way to Shambala.* NY: Anchor, 1981.

Bharati, Agehananda. "Actual and Ideal Himalayas: Hindu Views of the Mountains," in James F. Fisher ed. *Himalayan Anthropology: The Indo-Tibetan Interface.* The Hague: Mouton, 1978, 77-82.

Bishop, Peter. *The Myth of Shangri-La.* Berkeley: University of California Press, 1989.

Law, B.C. "The Himalaya Mountains," in *Indological Studies IV.* Allahabad: Jha Research Institute, 1954, 166-195.

Roerich, G.N. *The Blue Annals of gZhon-nu-dpal.* Calcutta, 1949.

Wylie, Turrell. "Tibetan Religious Geography of Nepal," *Serie Orientale Roma XLII*, 1970.

_____. "A Place Name Index to George N. Roerich's Translation of the Blue Annals" *Serie Orientale Roma XV*, 1957, 1-42.

Durga Shrine with Trident, Central Nepal

46

PART TWO:

HISTORY OF HIMALAYAN CIVILIZATIONS

Inscribed Ashokan Pillar, Lumbini

47

Sun Temple, Martand, Kashmir

Chapter 6

KASHMIR AND THE WESTERN HIMALAYAS

I. Definitions

A. Ambiguity of the term "Kashmir"
 1. Kashmir Valley
 2. Modern state of Jammu and Kashmir.

B. Western Himalayas includes Himachal Pradesh

C. The Modern State of Jammu and Kashmir
 1. Physical Geography
  a. location
  b. size and extent
   1. divisions: Azad Kashmir
   2. Jammu and Kashmir
 2. Topography
  a. mountains and plains
   1. lowlands
   2. Pir Panjal and Siwalik (Shivalekha) ranges
   3. the High Himalayas and Trans-Himalaya
   4. relation to Karakoram and Hindu Kush
  b. major rivers and river valleys
   1. Indus
   2. Jhelum (Vitasta)
   3. Ravi
   4. Chenab
   5. Sutlej
 3. Culture Areas
  a. sub-montane: Jammu and the Panjab Plains
  b. mid-montane pahari
  c. Kashmir Valley
  d. Tibetan Highlands
  e. Karakoram Highlands
 4. Political units at one time or another part of the state
  a. Northwest Kingdoms: Hunza, Gilgit, Chitral, Dir, Nagar.
  b. Ladakh
  c. Dardistan
  d. Kashmir Valley
  e. Jammu

5. Processes of State Formation
   a. military conquest and unification
   b. treaties
   c. Islamification
   d. colonial rule

D. Historical Areas
   1. Core Areas: continuous history from ancient times
      a. Panjab Plains
      b. the Kashmir Valley
   2. Peripheral areas: areas with little known ancient history, partially or unknown medieval/modern history
      a. mid-montane Pahari: Panjab hill states
      b. Tibetan highlands: Ladakh, Zanskar, Spiti, Lahul
      c. mid-montane Tibeto-Burman: Kulu
      d. the North-Western States: Hunza, etc.

II. Core Areas in Ancient Kashmir History (3000 BC-1200 AD)

A. Northern Panjab Plains
   1. Sources
      a. archaeological
      b. literary
   2. Geography
      a. lowlands
      b. salt ranges
      c. major rivers
         1. Indus
         2. Ravi
         3. Chenab
         4. Sutlej
      d. climate
         1. monsoon
         2. highland desert
   3. Prehistory
      a. paleolithic evidence
      b. neolithic evidence
      c. Indus Valley civilization: site at Manda, near Jammu
      d. Aryan culture
   4. Ancient Period: Textual Sources
      a. Ashokan inscriptions
      b. Kharosthi inscriptions and coinage
      c. Gupta inscriptions: coinage
      d. the Huns: inscriptional and textual evidence

B. The Kashmir Valley
   1. Sources
      a. archaeological
      b. literary
   2. Physical Geography
      a. altitude and area
         1. 5000 ft. above sea level
         2. area approximately 2000 sq. miles
      b. mountains
         1. surrounded by mountains on all sides
         2. prominent peaks:
            a. north: Nanga Parbat, 26,000 ft.
            b. east: Harmukh, 16,000 ft.
            c. south and west: Pir Panjal range, 15,000 ft.
      c. rivers: Jhelum river watershed
         1. ancient name: Vitasta
         2. drains the entire valley, exits at Baramula, 34 miles west of modern Srinagar
         3. rivers navigable, connected to glacial lakes
      d. trade routes
         1. main route of access to lower India and central Asian trade routes: via Baramula
         2. Zoji-la, to Ladakh
         3. Pahalgam, to the Amarnath Caves
         4. trade routes made the valley a mixed society, with Central Asians, Indians, Persians
      e. specific characteristics of the area:
         1. geographic features for the most part helped keep invaders out and preserved cultural autonomy
         2. the *karewas*
         3. the lake and canal system

III. History of Ancient Kashmir (3000 BC-1200 AD)

A. Prehistory
   1. Paleontology
      a. animal finds
      b. hominid finds
      c. paleolithic
         1. stray surface finds
         2. Bursahom
   2. Mythology: Origins, Sacred Geography, Sacred Time

a. sacred texts
1. *Nilamatapurana*
2. *Vitastamahatmya*
3. Kashmir *mahatmya* literature
a. almost each *tirtha* has a *mahatmya* in Sanskrit.
b. Stein lists over 50.
b. the major chronicles
1. *Rajatarangini* of Kalhana
2. *Rajatarangini* of Jonaraja
3. *Rajatarangini* of Srivara
c. textual structure of time and space
1. the *yugas*
2. Kashmir sacred geography
3. human time and sacred time
a. the beginning of human history
b. the end of human history
c. the royal eras used in Kashmir

B. The Ancient Period (to 1200 AD)
1. Historical sources
a. indigenous
1. epigraphy
2. Sanskrit inscriptions
3. Prakit inscriptions
b. Buddhist and Hindu textual tradition
c. numismatics
1. Kushan coinage
2. Hunnic coinage
3. later Kashmir coinage
d. art and archaeology
1. earliest sites
a. Pradhanadhisthana
b. Harwan
c. Parihasapura
d. Avantipura
e. Martand
2. early bronze and stone sculpture
e. Outside Sources
1. Indic texts from epic period refer to region
2. Tibetan Buddhist Histories
3. Chinese History: *Kin-pin*
4. European sources
a. Greek and other classical authors
b. Byzantine writers
c. Marco Polo

        d. Persian and Arabic sources: Abu-l-Fazl

        e. Mughul historians

        f. European travel accounts

2. Overview of the Early Dynastic Period

    a. early rulers

        1. Gonanda I and his successors

        2. Ashoka (250 BC)

        3. Jalauka

        4. the Kushan Kings: Hushka, Jushka, Kanishka (c. 50 BC-150 AD)

        5. Mihirakula

        6. Toramana

        7. the Karkota Dynasty (650-750 AD)

        8. the Utpala Dynasty (855-980 AD)

        9. first Lohara Dynasty (1101-1128 AD)

    b. political organization

        1. ancient political divisions

            a. Kramarajya (Kamraz)

            b. Madavarajya (Maraz)

            c. *visaya* or district

                1. traditionally Valley divided into 27 *visayas*

            d. extensive deserted village remains indicate relatively large ancient population

            e. city of Srinagar, the capital

                1. Puranadhisthana (Pandrethan)

                2. Srinagara

                3. Pravarapura

            f. site of royal Palace

                1. transfer of palace by King Ananta (1028-63) to "vicinity of Sadasiva shrine"

            g. watch stations and passes

                1. *dranga*

                2. *dvara*

3. Major Events and Rulers

    a. era of Kushan dominance (2nd Cent)

    b. Hunnic invasions (5th Cent)

    c. Karkota Dynasty (7th Cent)

        1. first indigenous centralization of power

        2. visit of Hsuang Tsang (7th Cent)

    d. Lalitaditya (730-750)

        1. invaded and ruled large areas of North India

        2. patron of Brahmins and Buddhists

        3. built Sun temple at Martand

    e. Avantivarman (855-883)

      1. improvements in irrigation by Suyya
         a. removed threat of floods
         b. converted dry uplands to productive croplands
         c. created agricultural surpluses
   f. Lohara Dynasty (10th Cent)
      1. continued expansion of irrigation
      2. political life dominated by rivalry between central authority of king and feudatory *damaras*

4. Social and Economic Organization
   a. organized according to castes
      1. *Brahmans*: priests, ministers of state, generals
      2. *damaras*: feudatories, landed with aristocracy
      3. *shrestins, vanikas*: merchants active in Valley and Central Asia, selling wool, glass, etc.
      4. low castes:
         a. *nisada*, hunters
         b. *domba*, musicians
         c. *candala*, sweepers
   b. agriculture
      1. majority of population in agriculture
      2. key resources
         a. rich clay soil
         b. saffron
         c. abundant water
   c. relations with adjacent areas
      1. ancient kingdoms of Gandhara and Bactria
      2. the Swat Valley
      3. Greek influence through Alexandrine invasions
      4. relations with Tibet
         a. according to tradition, Tibetan king sent Thon-mi to Kashmir to devise a script for Tibetan
         b. other influences brought by Tibetans in Kashmir and Kashmiris in Tibet, especially in Buddhist doctrine, ordination lineages, art
         c. Ladakh area linked to the Kashmir Valley
      5. relations with the plains of India
         a. ancient civilization in the plains: Indus and "Aryan" civilization
         b. the spread of Buddhism
         c. the Maurya, Kushan, Gupta empires

5. Language and Literature
   a. chief language is Sanskrit
   b. early history of Kashmiri is unknown, though it is considered to be an Indo-Aryan language.
   c. chief authors of ancient Kashmir:

1. philosophical and religious
    a. Utpaladeva
    b. Abhinavagupta (975-1025 AD)
    c. Anandavardhana
    d. Ksemaraja
2. belle-lettres
    a. Ksemendra (c. 1000 AD)
    b. Somadeva (c. 1080 AD)
    c. Bilhana (c. 1100 AD)
    d. Kalhana (c. 1140 AD)

6. Religion
    a. Buddhist Kashmir
        1. lack of independent corroboration of Buddhist literature and the problem of sectarian bias
        2. Ashokan era
            a. later travelers mention four stupas built in the Valley by Ashoka
            b. Hinayana accounts of third Buddhist council state that Ashoka sent Bhiksu Majjhantika to Kashmir and that he converted the *nagas*
        3. the Kushan era
            a. Sarvastivada tradition states that the fourth Buddhist council was held in Kashmir by Kanishka; council codified the Sanskrit Buddhist canon; commentary on these texts, the *Mahavibhasa*, also composed there
            b. Kushan influence in the Valley strong
            c. Valley became center of the Sarvastivada school
                1. analyzed the world according to seventy-five constituents
                2. accepted reality of past, present, and future
                3. doctrine of two truths
                4. forerunner of *Mahayana*
        4. Gupta Era
            a. Kashmir recognized as a center of Buddhism; linked to *Mahayana* and its origins.
            b. monks from all over India, Central Asia, even China traveled there for study
            c. Kashmir monks spread Buddhism to China
                1. Kumarajiva (400 AD) invited by Emperor; translated 106 texts into Chinese

55

5. Karkota era
    a. Hsuan Tsang's account
        1. description of scholars, preachers, monasteries
        2. "100 *viharas*, 5,000 monks"
    b. Hinduism in Ancient Kashmir
        1. according to Hsuan Tsang, Hinduism is stronger than Buddhism in places
        2. continuity of Shiva worship from early times
        3. Valley also a center of Hindu learning and study; students from as far away as Bengal, Bihar, the south of India, come to study
        4. Trika Saivism, a sectarian Hindu movement develops with its chief center in Kashmir
            a. founder: Vasugupta, 9th century teacher
            b. teachings: highest reality is monistic; expressed in terms of Shiva; last stage of salvation not attained without Shiva's grace
        5. unconfirmed tradition includes visits of Sankaracharya
        6. the place of Vaisnavism
7. Art and Archaeology
    a. architecture: chief sites
        1. Avantipur
        2. Martand
        3. Parihasapura
    b. sculpture
        1. little bronze sculpture remains
        2. oldest stone sculptures
        3. Kushan terracottas
        4. ivory carvings
    c. no ancient paintings survive in the Valley

III. The Middle Period: 1200-1800 AD

A. Definition of Core Areas
    1. Kashmir Valley
    2. The hill kingdoms of the Northwest
    3. The hill kingdoms east of Kashmir

B. Historical Sources
   1. Epigraphy
      a. the Sarada inscriptions
      b. the inscriptions of Chamba and the Himalayan hill kingdoms
   2. Numismatics: coins of the Kashmir kings
   3. Art and Archaeology
      a. late Hindu-Buddhist remains
      b. early Islamic architecture
   4. Outside Sources
      a. India
         1. textual references
         2. Islamic accounts
            a. Mughul historians
            b. diaries
            c. travellers' accounts
      b. Tibetan-Buddhist histories
      c. Chinese annals
      d. early European travel accounts
   5. Local Sources
      a. later chronicles of Jonaraja and Srivara
      b. Kashmiri literature

C. Major Rulers and Events
   1. The coming of Muslim rule
      a. conquest by Shah Mir in 1337 began rule by Muslim kings that lasted until 1819. Rulers' policy varies between tolerance to persecution of non-Muslims
      b. Sikander (ruled 1390-1414)
         1. made excursions into north India
         2. Islam entered aggressive phase
         3. population given first choice of conversion or emigration; later choice of conversion or death
         4. the minister of Sikander, Subhatta, a converted Brahman, chief architect of fanatical policies
      c. Zain ud Abidin (ruled 1421-1472)
         1. era of public works and state-run industries
         2. toleration of Hinduism
            a. Brahmins repatriated and some land restored
            b. Buddhists and Hindus allowed to hold government posts
            c. *puja*, pilgrimage, and cremation allowed
         3. military excursions into Sind and western Tibet
         4. era of cultural richness
      d. Haidar Shah

1. returns to policies of religious persecution and civil strife
2. intense period of struggle within Kashmir
   2. Kashmir under Mughul rule (1587-1739)
      a. the end of Kashmiri independence
      b. once integrated into the empire, Mughal rulers exercise paternal care over the Valley
      c. few internal conflicts
      d. alternating policies of tolerance and persecution
         1. Akbar
         2. Jahangir
         3. Aurangzeb
   3. Kashmir under Afghan rule (1752-1819)
      a. Afghan invasions and decline of the Mughuls
      b. invasions of Nadir Shah
      c. severing of communications between Kashmir and the Mughul court
      d. invasion of Ahmad Khan, founder of Durani dynasty
      e. Kashmir ruled by governors appointed in Kabul
      f. harsh, oppressive rule of Afghans ends only in 1819

D. Social and Economic Organization
   1. Destruction of Hindu-Buddhist synthesis
      a. physical destruction of major monuments completed by beginning of 15th century
      b. society estimated to be ninety percent Muslim by end of same period
      c. Hindus remain isolated minority
      d. Buddhism disappears
   2. Integration of Kashmir into Mughul Empire
      a. end of Kashmir independence from north India
      b. governors appointed by Mughuls
      c. establishment of imperial monopolies in saffron and other important commodities
      d. emperor, governor, and the people of Kashmir: their roles at time of crisis
         1. famine
         2. plague
         3. invasion
         4. building and destruction: the new use of ancient monuments

E. Language and Literature
   1. The rise of Kashmiri as a vernacular and literary language
      a. Poetry of Lal Dedh

2. Continued use of Sanskrit

3. Influence of Persian and Arabic

4. the rise of Urdu

F. Art and Archaeology

1. Muslim architecture in Kashmir

    a. continuity of North Indian traditions

    b. chief monuments

        1. Shalimar gardens

        2. Shah Hamdam Masjid

        3. Khakah Masjid

2. Crafts

    a. rug design

    b. papier mache

    c. silver and other metal work

    d. wood and ivory carving

Central Mosque, Srinagar

IV. The Modern Period: 1800 AD -- Present

A. Definition of the Area: Kashmir Valley, kingdom of Jammu, Ladakh

B. Historical Sources
1. Epigraphy
2. Numismatics
3. Art and Archaeology
4. Outside sources
   a. Indian
   b. Tibetan
   c. Chinese
   d. European travellers
   e. British accounts and archives
5. Local sources
   a. government archives
   b. local histories

C. Political History
1. Sikh conquest of Ranjit Singh: 1819
   a. the first non-Muslim rule since the 14th century
   b. situation of Hindu minority improves
   c. Hindus have new role in government
   d. British support Sikh states as buffer with Afghanistan
2. Death of Ranjit Singh in 1839
3. Weakening of Sikh State
4. First and Second Sikh Wars with the British
5. The Rise of the Dogras
   a. the Dogras, a Hindu group, ruled Jammu at the end of Mughul period, conquered by Sikhs in 1808 led by Ranjit Singh
   b. Gulab Singh, a Dogra soldier from a family of Jammu that initially resisted the Sikh army, rose from ordinary soldier to become *raja* of Jammu
   c. conquest of Ladakh by Gulab Singh, 1834
   d. Dogras move into western Tibet, but are defeated by Tibetan army and pursued to Ladakh; in Ladakh, Dogras win battle and hostilities cease, 1841
   e. Treaty of Amritsar, 1846. Kashmir ceded to Gulab Singh and the Dogras. Gulab Singh becomes first Hindu *maharaja* of modern period.
   f. state of Jammu and Kashmir ruled by Dogras until 1947

6. Impact of Colonialism
   a. increasing role of British in Kashmiri affairs after the death of Gulab Singh in 1858
   b. British Residency established in Kashmir in 1885
   c. Pratap Singh, Maharaja of Kashmir, signs Edict of Resignation in 1889, establishing Council of Regency subject to control of Resident
   d. Council terminated in 1905
   e. State Council of Ministers formed in 1922

D. Social and Economic Organization
   1. Sikh-Dogra rule gives Hindus new advantage
   2. British support Hindu elite; Hindus hold key administrative posts
   3. British attempts at social and economic reforms
      a. The Settlement (1887-93)
   4. Muslim organization and grievances

E. Political Organization: The Emergence of Political Parties
   1. The rise of Sheikh Abdullah
   2. The All-Jammu and Kashmir Muslim Conference, 1932-39
   3. All-Jammu and Kashmir National Conference
   4. Hindu and Muslim rivalries

F. The Independence of India and the status of Kashmir
   1. The creation of India and Pakistan, 1947
   2. The accession of Kashmir to India
   3. The outbreak of hostilities between India and Pakistan
   4. Establishment of a ceasefire line
   5. Hostilities over the last thirty years
      a. successive wars between India and Pakistan: 1965, 1971
      b. the career of Sheikh Abdullah
         1. his imprisonment
         2. his release and chief ministership
   6. Line of control defined between India and Pakistan in 1972 along cease-fire line: 46,976 sq. mi.to Pakistan in the north and west and 38,829 sq. mi. India. Bulk of wealth and population on Indian side.

G. Kashmir Divided
   1. Azad Kashmir ("Free Kashmir") of Pakistan
   2. The Indian state of Kashmir

H. Recent Events
   1. Big power rivalry in Kashmir
   2. Kashmir after the Soviet invasion of Afghanistan, 1979

3. Continuing tension between India and Pakistan exacerbated by Chinese activity in Tibet, Sinkiang, and the borders of Ladakh
4. Death of Sheikh Abdullah, 1984
5. Farooq Abdullah becomes chief minister but is dismissed by Governor Jag Mohan, 1984
6. Rising feelings of separatism in a population dissatisfied both with Congress and National Conference politics
7. Farooq becomes chief minister again after elections, 1987
8. Popular dissatisfaction with election results due to feeling that results were manipulated by Congress and National Conference, 1987.
9. Widespread riots. Murder of Vice-Chancellor of Kashmir University and Imam Mulvi Muhammad Farooq; Srinagar closed, 1987.
10. Buddhists of Ladakh demand separation from Jammu and Kashmir and formation of a Union Territory of Ladakh. Islamic militants control large urban enclaves and move freely in the countryside, 1989.
11. Islamic movement develops into full separatist agitation; many militants trained in Pakistan
12. Violence continues and 2200 people killed. Kidnapping miltant separatists of daughter of Maufti Mohammad Sayeed, Indian Home Minister, demanding release of five imprisoned political activists. Prime Minister V.P. Singh releases them, 1990.
13. Indian military suppresses movement: thousands arrested during house to house searches; foreign press banned. Farooq resigns and Jag Mohan appointed governor for second time. Legislature dismissed.
14. Mass protests, heavy crackdown by Indian military. Human rights violations charged against Indian Government. Jag Mohan recalled, replaced by G.S. Saxena. Presidential rule, 1990.
15. Continued repressive rule, 1991-4. Economic hardship resulting in migration of many to Delhi and other population centers in India.
16. Hindu Pandits flee to refugee camps in the Jammu hills
17. Hindu pilgrims attacked on the 1993 pilgrimage to Amarnath
18. Distruction of town Charar-i-Sharif and its monuments, May 1995

Recommended Readings and References

Ancient Period

Basham, A. L. "The Kashmir Chronicle," in C. H. Phillips ed. *Historians of India, Pakistan, and Ceylon*. London: Oxford University Press, 1961, 57-65.

Basu, Arabinda. "Kashmir Saivism," *Cultural Heritage of India IV*, 1956, 79-97.

de Terra, Helmut. "The Megaliths of Bursahom, Kashmir, a New Prehistoric Civilization from India," *Proceedings of the American Philosophical Society* 85 (Nov. 1941-Sept. 1942).

Dutt, Nalinaksha. "Buddhism in Kashmir," *Gilgit Manuscripts I*. Srinagar, 1939, 3-45.

Goetz, Hermann. "The Sun Temple of Martand," in *Studies in the History and Art of Kashmir and the Indian Himalaya*. Wiesbaden: Otto Harrassowitz, 1969.

Jettmar, Karl ed. *Antiquities of Northern Pakistan*. Mainz: Heidelberg Academy, 1989.

Kumari, Ved ed.. *The Nilamata Purana*. Vol. II (J & K). Srinagar: Academy of Art, Cultures and Languages, 1973.

Polo, Marco. "On the Province of Kashmir." In *The Book of Ser Marco Polo the Venetian Concerning the Kingdoms and Marvels of the East*. New York: Charles Scribners and Sons, 1903.

Sanderson, Alexis. "Abhinavagupta," in Mircea Eliade ed. *The Encyclopaedia of Religion*, I. New York: Macmillan, 1987, 8-9.

Sankalia, H.D. "New Evidence for Early Man in Kashmir," *Current Anthopology 12* (4/5), 1971, 558-562.

Stein, M.A. (trans.) *Kalhana's Rajatarangani*. Vol. 1. New Delhi: Motilal Banarsidass, 1979.

_____. "Archaeological Notes from the Hindu Kush Religion," *Journal of the Royal Asiatic Society* 1994, 5-24.

Tucci, Giuseppe. "Preliminary Report on an Archaeological Survey in Swat," *East and West 9* (4), 1958, 279-328.

Vogel, J. (ed.). "Antiquities of Chamba State," Vol. 1, Ch. V. *Archaeological Survey*, New Imperial Series 36, 1911.

Middle Period

Beveridge, Henry (ed.). *The Tuluk-i-Jahangiri, or Memoirs of Jahangir*. Trans. by Alexander Rogers. 2nd ed. Munshiram Manoharlal, 1968.

Goetz, Hermann. "History of Chamba in Mughal and Sikh Times," *Journal of Indian History 31*, 1953, 136-156.

_____. "History of Chamba State in the Later Middle Ages," *Journal of Indian History 30,* 1952: 293-308.

Haig, Sir Worsley. "The Kingdom of Kashmir," in *The Cambridge History of India*. Vol III. New Delhi, 1958.

Kosambi, D.D. "Origins of Feudalism in Kashmir," *Journal of the Asiatic Society of Bombay* 31/32, 1956/57, 108-120.

Petech, Luciano. *The Kingdom of Ladakh*. Rome: Istituto Italiano per Il Medio ed Estremo Oriente, 1977.

Modern Period

Allen, Nigel J.R. ed. *North Pakistan: Karakorum Conquered*. New York: St. Martins Press, 1994.

Das Gupta, Jyoti Bhusan. *Jammu and Kashmir*. The Hague: Mouton, 1968.

Huttenback, Robert. "Gulab Singh and the Creation of the Dogra State of Jammu, Kashmir, and Ladakh," *Journal of Asian Studies* 20 (4), 1961: 477-88.

Lamb, Alastair. *Crisis in Kashmir*. London, 1966.

_____. *Britain and Chinese Central Asia: The Road to Lhasa 1757 to 1905*. London: Routledge and Kegan Paul, 1960.

Singh, Khushwant. *Ranjit Singh: Maharaja of Punjab*. London: George Allen, 1962.

Wangu, Madhu Bazaz. "Hermeneutics of a Kashmiri Mahatmya Text in Context," in Jeffrey R. Timm ed. *Texts in Context*. New York: State University of New York Press, 1992.

Newberg, Paula. *Double Betrayal*. Washington DC: Carnegie Endowment for World Peace, 1995.

Mosque in Chitral

Vishvarupa Vishnu and other Sculptures, Changu Narayan

Chapter 7

NEPAL AND THE CENTRAL HIMALAYAS

I. Definitions

    A. Modern ambiguity of the designation "Nepal"
        1. Traditional definition applies only to Kathmandu Valley
        2. Modern state of Nepal (post 1815)

    B. Central Himalayas
        1. Areas west of state of Nepal
            a. Kumaon
            b. Garhwal
        2. Areas east of Nepal
            a. Sikkim
            b. Darjeeling

    C. The Modern Kingdom of Nepal
        1. Physical Geography
            a. location
            b. size and extent
        2. Topography
            a. mountains and plains
                1. lowlands (Tarai)
                2. Mahabharata Chain
                3. the High Himalayas
            b. major rivers and river valleys
                1. Mahakali
                2. Karnali
                3. Kali Gandaki
                4. Bagmati
                5. Kosi
                6. Arun
                7. Mechi
        3. Culture Areas
            a. sub-montane or Terai
            b. mid-montane Pahari
            c. mid-montane Tibeto-Burman
            d. Kathmandu Valley (also called Nepal Valley)
            e. Tibetan Highlands
        4. Political units unified in the kingdom of Nepal

      a. *Chaubisi rajya*

      b. *Baisi rajya*

      c. Mustang

      d. Gorkha

      e. Nepal Valley kingdoms and posessions

      f. Makwanpur

      g. Tarai kingdoms of Tirhut and Mithila

      h. Limbuvan

5. Processes of State Formation

      a. military conquest

      b. treaties

      c. legal unification

      d. autocratic rule

      e. xenophobia as national policy: "Forbidden Kingdom"

      f. Hinduization

      g. Sanskritization

      h. language uniformity: Nepali as national language

D. Historical Areas

  1. Core Areas: continuous history from ancient times

      a. Kingdoms of Tarai

      b. Nepal Valley

  2. Peripheral areas: areas with little known ancient history, partially or unknown medieval/modern history

      a. mid-montane Pahari

          1. *Chaubisi* and *Baisi rajyas*

          2. Gorkha

      b. Tibetan Highlands: Humla, Mustang Dolpo, Langtang, Solu

      c. mid-montane Tibeto-Burman territories of the Rai, Limbu, Tamang

II. Ancient History of Nepal and Core Areas (1000 BC--1200 AD)

A. Tarai: Indian and Nepalese

  1. Sources

      a. archaeological

      b. literary

  2. Physical Geography

      a. lowlands

      b. forest belt

      c. rivers

          1. Gandaki

          2. Bagmati

          3. Ganges as border

3. Climate
    a. monsoon
    b. subtropical
    c. malaria as critical historical factor

B. The Nepal Valley
    1. Sources
        a. archaeological
        b. literary
    2. Physical Geography
        a. average altitude for the Valley: 4,600 ft. above sea level
        b. surrounding mountains: average 8-10,000 ft.
            1. North: Shivapuri
            2. East: Pulchowki
            3. South: Chandragiri
            4. West: Nagarjuna
        c. rivers
            1. Major Rivers: Vishnumati, Hanumante, Dhobi Khola, Manohara, Bagmati
            2. Bagmati, tributary of the Ganges, drains entire valley
        d. trade routes
            1. two main routes to Tibet
                a. north via Nuvakot and Kuti
                b. east and north via Sankhu and Kodari
            2. south via Makwanpur
            3. valley connected by trade to nearby hill areas in east and west
        e. specific characteristics of the area
            1. valley a slightly elliptical bowl, 20 miles by 15 miles; second in population size only to Kashmir in the Himalayas
            2. why the Valley developed as an important center of civilization
                a. rich, fertile soil and abundant water supply
                b. valley and entrepot along popular north-south trade route with relatively low Himalayan passes; middlemen traders centered in Valley, going south in the cold season, and north in the warm season.
                c. isolation afforded by the mountains
                d. malarial Tarai kept Valley independent from southern states
    3. Prehistory
        a. paleontology
            1. human remains
            2. animal remains

    b. paleolithic sites
        1. stray surface finds
            a. Dumakhal
            b. Budhanilkanth
    c. neolithic sites
        1. stray surface finds
            a. Dumakhal
            b. Budhanilkanth
            c. Lubhu
4. Mythology: Origins, Sacred Geography, Sacred Time
    a. sacred texts
        1. *Himavat Khanda*
        2. *Pashupati Purana*
        3. *Vagmati Mahatmya*
        4. *Nepalamahatmya*
        5. *Svayambhu Purana*
    b. the Chronicles (*vamshavali*)
        1. *Gopalarajavamshavali* and cognate works
        2. Wright chronicle and cognate works
        3. the chronicle of Siddhi Narayana and cognate works
    c. the structure of sacred time and space
        1. the *yugas*
        2. Nepalese sacred geography
        3. human time and sacred time
            a. the beginning of dynastic history
            b. the end of human history
            c. the human eras used in Nepal

III. The Early Historic Period: 300-1200 AD

A. Historical Sources

1. Indigenous
    a. epigraphy
        1. almost 200 inscriptions in Sanskrit: 464-878 AD
        2. Khas inscriptions of Western Nepal 9th and 12th
           centuries: Dullu, Dailekh, and Jumla
    b. numismatics
        1. Pashupati series
        2. Mananka
        3. Gunanka
        4. coins of Amshuvarman
        5. coins of Jishnugupta
    c. art and archaeology
        1. earliest stone sculptures found in Hadigaun

       2. few bronzes remain of period

       3. pottery related to that of north Indian sites at Ahicchatra, Vaishali and other sites

       4. earliest sites at Dumakhal, Hadigaun, and Dhumbarahi

  2. Outside Sources

    a. Indian references in *Puranas*, *Arthasastra*, and some Buddhist texts

    b. Tibetan Buddhist histories

    c. Chinese histories

B. Licchavi Period (400-800 A.D)

1. No firm evidence as yet links the dynasty that ruled Nepal to the family from Vaishali, but the likelihood of a connection is high: Nepalese Licchavis appeared to have been an Indian or Indicized elite

2. Licchavi capital possibly near Pashupatinath, at site close to modern Hadigaun; palaces named Managriha, Kailashakuta, and Bhadradivasa

3. Political organization

    a. generally conforms to that of Northern India: absolute monarchy that claimed ownership of all land

    b. local units of administration

       1. collect taxes, organize labor forces, adjudicate minor disputes

       2. major administrative units

          a. *lingval, mapcok, kuther, sulya, bhatta*, were chief administrative units

          b. *grama, dranga, taladranga* were important village and town designations

    c. major settlements:

       1. Daksinakoligrama (Kathmandu)

       2. Yupagramadranga (Patan)

       3. Khrmprmgrama (Bhaktapur)

    d. many village names recognizable from inscriptions

    e. military under king and commander-in-chief (*mahasenapati*)

    f. other officers: *mahadandanayaka*; *catabhata*; *mahasamanta*

4. Unconfirmed ancient traditions

    a. all originate from later periods and remain unsubstantiated by archaeological evidence or other contemporary sources

    b. legendary Nepalese Dynasties

       1. Gopala

       2. Mahisapala

       3. Kirata

       4. Abhira or Abhiragupta

    c. Buddhist accounts

       1. Shakyamuni Buddha visited the Kathmandu Valley

       2. the Buddha's close disciple Ananda returned from a journey to Nepal due to "hardships of the trail"

       3. visit of King Ashoka and building of the four stupas of Patan lacks ancient epigraphic evidence

       4. King Ashoka's daughter Carumati visited the valley. married a local prince, and founded a monastery at Cha Bahil

       5. Vasubandhu, the great Buddhist master of the Yogacara school (200 AD), died in Nepal (Tibetan historical tradition)

    d. death of the Jain saint Bhadrabahu in Nepal

    e. Hindu-Buddhist account: visit of Shankaracarya to the Valley

5. Important Rulers

    a. King Manadeva (464-505 AD)

       1. gained control of hill areas outside the Valley

       2. erected pillar at Changu Narayan

       3. issued coinage

       4. first Licchavi kind of whom we have contemporary literary evidence and coinage

    b. King Amshuvarman (605-621 AD)

       1. not of Licchavi family

       2. appears to have been a *mahasamanta* or great vassal of Licchavi kings

       3. ruled jointly with the Licchavi Shivadeva, then usurped the throne

       4. strong ruler and cultural patron

       5. known to Chinese pilgrims and mentioned in Tibetan and East Asian sources

    c. Other important monarchs

       1. Jishnugupta (631-633 AD)

       2. Narendradeva (643-685 AD)

       3. Jayadeva (713-733 AD)

    d. relations with adjacent areas

       1. close relations with Gupta Empire

       2. Gupta capital of Pataliputra only 150 miles from Valley

       3. trade relations with Vaishali and other major North Indian centers

       4. artistic influences from India strong

6. Religion

    a. pluralism and tolerance were general features of the religious life

    b. Sanskrit as official language

    c. royal patrons supported all religious sects but were most generous toward Brahmanical Hinduism

d. Hindu and Buddhist traditions were differentiated in some areas, similar in many others; the Chinese pilgrim Hsuang Tsang reports hearing that "*viharas* and Hindu temples were placed side by side"

e. Buddhism
   1. Buddhism present from the beginning of the period, and its appearance seems to conform to the spectrum of traditions existing at this same time in North India, with *Hinayana, Mahayana,* and *Vajrayana* expressions
   2. according to the Tibetan historian Taranatha's account, "in the small country of Nepal, the *Dharma* was very active. Both the *Sravakayana* and the *Mahayana* were very strong, but kings and nobles were especially generous to the *Mahayana*"
   3. the *bhikshuni sangha* (of the Caturvimsha school) survived there until Amshuvarman's era
   4. where kings gave royal grants, Buddhist *sangha* had responsibility to administer entire villages
   5. Patronage by caravan merchants

f. Hinduism
   1. earliest inscriptions indicate rulers were Hindus, supporting Brahman rituals, Brahmanical codes, and patronizing both Vaishnavas and Shaivites
   2. state of Hinduism's evolution seems similiar to tradition elsewhere in north India
   3. caste concepts and stages of life (*varnashrama*) also evident, indicating high caste dominance
   4. chief religious shrines:
      a. Pashupati
      b. Changunarayan
      c. Budhanilkantha
      d. Satyanarayan
   5. practice of *sati*
      a. inscriptional evidence indicates this practice as optional for women of ruling families
      b. extent of practice unknown among other classes
   6. Hinduism continues to grow through royal patronage and Brahmanical influence

7. Literature
   a. ancient literature of Nepal is no longer extant
   b. most texts are thought to have been composed outside the valley
   c. oldest mss. date from 10th or 11th century
   d. Budhasvamin's *Brhatslokasamgraha* thought to have been composed in Nepal (7th-8th century)

8. Art and archaeology
    a. architecture
        1. oldest monuments
            a. *stupas*
            b. temples
            c. *viharas*
        2. problem of dating given accretive traditions
    b. sculpture
        1. earliest figures of Hindu, Buddhist, and mother goddesses
        2. dating mostly conjectural, e.g. Hadigau *yaksa/bodhisattva*, circa first century AD

C. Post-Licchavi Period (800-1200 AD)

1. Epigraphical and numismatic record ends
2. Earliest colophons of manuscripts in a new era, called *"Nepal Samvat"* ; it commences in 879 AD
3. Numismatic record appears to end for almost five hundred years
4. Some rulers continue to bear Sanskritic names ending in "*deva*", but little evidence is available about their origins or connections
5. Almost no information about society
6. Possible disputes among ruling elites that ultimately lead to the formation of Malla dynasty, the major dynasty of the medieval period
7. Colophons indicate existence of the chief cities of the Valley: Kasthamandapa, Lalitapattana, and Bhaktagrama
8. Social and economic organization
    a. most inhabitants agriculturalists
    b. trade between North India and Tibet is channeled more and more through Valley
        1. traders waited in valley for the cold season for going south through malarial Tarai and for the summer season when the passes opened to the north
        2. local trading population engaged in middleman activities, warehousing goods, sending caravans
    c. artisan communities specializing in all media--stone, metal casting, woodworking, manuscript painting, temple building
9. Relations with adjacent areas
    a. Buddhist teachers continue to visit Valley from chief centers of India and Tibet
    b. Pala influence on Nepalese arts
10. Language
    a. archaic form of the language now spoken in the Valley, now called Nepal: *"Bhasa"* or "*Newa Bhay*" by modern speakers-- "Newari" as a Westernized neologism--was likely in use by the end of this period at the latest
    b. Sanskrit endured in textual writings

III. Nepal in the Middle Period: 1200--1800 AD

A. Core Areas
   1. Kathmandu Valley
   2. Kingdoms of Western Nepal
      a. the Mallas: formation, extent, ethos
      b. state covering areas of western Tibet and Nepal, with joint capitals at Guge and site near Jumla
   3. Kingdoms of the Tarai
      a. Mithala
      b. Makwanpur
      c. Vijapur

B. Historical Sources
   1. Epigraphy
      a. Malla inscriptions of the Kathmandu Valley
         1. stone
         2. copper
         3. palm
         4. mss. colophons
         5. coinage
         6. other local sources
      b. medieval texts
         1. chronicles
         2. *Nepalamhatmya*: a religious geography of the Kathmandu Valley
         3. *Svayambhupurana*: account of the origins of the main Newar Buddhist shrines, Valley, and original inhabitants of Nepal
         4. *thyasaphus*: diaries and records of various individuals
   2. Art and Archaeology
      a. evolution of chief medieval styles
         1. architecture
         2. sculpture
         3. painting
         4. domestic art
   3. Folklore
   4. Outside Sources
      a. Indian
      b. Tibetan
      c. Chinese
      d. European
         1. travel accounts
         2. Catholic missionaries
         3. English travelers

C. The Early Mallas of the Nepal Valley
  1. "Malla" is title of honor in many places in India
  2. Early period of consolidation not well documented; time of families vying for power, local autonomy; dominant factions may have come from Mithila; among dominant groups of the Valley: the Ramavardhanas
  3. Rudra Malla of Banepa (early 1300s)
     a. eclipses power of "king"
     b. his descendants dominate later events
  4. Sthiti Malla (1382-1395)
     a. family origins possibly in Mithila
     b. forced other nobles in the Valley to concede his supreme standing, but allowed *mahapatras*-- "city leaders"--to retain power
        1. Kathmandu
        2. Patan
        3. Ramavardhanas of Banepa
           a. once posed as "Kings of Nepal" during misson by a Chinese ambassador from the Ming Court
           b. patrons of Valley shrines
           c. reputed in local traditions to have created and enforced caste laws that brought Valley society more in conformity with Indian Brahmanical standards.
           d. first king to identify himself with "Narayana", i.e. Vishnu
           e. bequeathed throne to three sons but two died, leaving single heir
  5. Jyotir Malla (1395-1427)
  6. Yaksha Malla (1428-1482)
     a. reduced Banepa's powers in Valley affairs
     b. made expeditions outside the Valley to secure frontiers, though extent is not known
     c. widescale patronage, especially in temples, water tanks, public works
     d. at end of term, grew restless and bequeathed his kingdom to three sons in three divisions:
        1. Kathmandu, Bhaktapur, Banepa
        2. Patan maintained independence under *mahapatra* rule until 1600, when it returned to direct Malla rule

Inscribed Stone Pillar, Dullu, Western Nepal

श्रीमहाराजकुमारीमहीन्द्रमल्ल

Painting of King Mihindra Malla

78

D. The Era of the Three Malla Kingdoms (1482-1769)
1. Kings of Bhaktapur controlled areas in the Valley east of the Hanumante, reaching to the Banepa Valley and as far east as the Sun Kosi River
2. Kings of Kathmandu controlled all areas north of the Bagmati, reaching to the Trisuli River
3. Kings of Patan controlled areas south of the Valley, including Kirtipur, Pharping, Chobar
4. Political Organization
   a. each town a walled city organized around a central palace, with high castes in the center, lower castes nearer the walls, untouchables outside the walls.
   b. officials at the courts were given land grants in exchange for their official duties
   c. though kinship ties linked all three, relations between the centers were usually antagonistic, unpleasant, marked by petty intrigues and occasional warfare
   d. rivalries between the competing centers supported extensive cultural employment, but weakened the Valley militarily, culminating in conquest by outsiders
   e. other villages and towns existed as satellites of the major kingdoms
5. Pratap Malla of Kathmandu (1641-1674)
   a. height of prosperity during his reign
   b. enlarged Hanuman Dhoka Palace
   c. avid patron of the arts and styled himself "Kavindra", lord among poets
   d. in inscriptions he calls himself: "In the handling of weapons, reading the Shastras, singing of songs, and in all fields execellent, King of Kings, chief of Nepal, extremely clever, poet laureate, Jaya Pratap Malla Deva"
6. Jaya Prakash Malla of Kathmandu (1735-1768)
   a. last Malla king of Kathmandu
   b. plundered the Pashupati treasure house to fight the Gorkha army
   c. attempted to secure English aid against Gorkha

E. The Shah Conquest
1. Background
   a. in 1559, a small hill town later known as Gorkha comes under rule of the Shah family
   b. forms alliance with surrounding tribes and kingdoms
2. Led by Prithvi Narayan Shah, Gorkha armies methodically cut off the Valley's trade routes, then conquered the major cities one by one, effectively playing on caste and city rivalries.

3. Entire Valley falls to the Gorkha armies by 1769
4. Expulsion of Capuchins

F. Social and Economic Organization
   1. Survivals from Licchavi times: *gosthis, pancalis*, trading castes.
   2. Malla legal codes influenced society toward increasing conformity with Brahmanical laws
   3. Ethnographic history by groups
      a. migration into the Valley by refugees from Muslim conquest and rule, especially Hindu royalty and Buddhist monks is assumed and likely, but historical data lacking
      b. in-migration of Pahari peoples
         1. steady migration of Indo-Aryan speaking peoples east into the Valley
         2. Nepali important language of Valley by 17th century. Language know as Khaskura or Parbatiya.
         3. Parbatiya speakers presumably lived outside the towns in ethnically homogenious villages

G. Connections with Adjacent Areas
   1. Relations with Mithila to the south had strong impact on Valley culture and society
   2. Relations with the Moghul Empire (1526-1858)
      a. Malla courts adopted Moghul dress, including ornaments and personal weapons
      b. Persian/Arabic vocabulary in local languages
      c. legal and administrative norms emulated
      d. Mulims in marketplace
      e. the influence of the Rajput Kingdoms
      f. absence of data from Moghul sources
   3. Relations with Tibet
      a. trade with central Tibet increased throughout the era, a source of wealth for the traders and and for the Newar kings who taxed the trade; traders from the Valley sent goods in both directions across the Nepal-Tibet frontier, and stationed agents to create a trade network that extended to all major settlements in central Tibet, reaching west to Ladakh
      b. Newars controlled many sectors of Tibetan economy
      c. Newar artisans worked widely in Tibet
         1. Arniko achieved fame in Tibet and later at the imperial court in China
         2. other architects and artisans helped build new monasteries
      d. the networks of Tibetan Buddhism reached into the Kathmandu Valley and likely influenced local Buddhist traditions
      e. ties with Bhutan develop from 1650 until Rana rule

4. Relations with Hill Areas
    a. some ethnic groups from the adjacent mid-hills served in the Malla courts as mercenaries
    b. migration by Pahari peoples into the Valley periphery led to new kinship networks and development of politically significant connections

H. Language

1. Emergence of Nepal Bhasa (i.e. "Newari") as court language, medium of literary composition, and inscriptions
    a. beginning of translation into Newari of major religious texts.
        1. Newari Hindu literature
        2. Newari Buddhist literature
    b. the influence of Sanskrit on Newari
    c. the emergence of "Khas Kura" or Parbatiya (Nepali)
2. Maithili language spoken in Malla courts, especially poetry and drama

I. Religion

1. Competition between the Three Kingdoms resulted in highly energetic cultural life as seen in:
    a. monument building that employed architects, stone and wood carvers, metalworkers (casting, repousee, ornament-makers), and priests
    b. literary activity that supported scholars copying old texts and making original compositions in Sanskrit, Newari and Maithili
    c. painters working in temple decoration and in miniature styles of North India
    d. performing arts in dance, drama, music
2. Malla patronage
    a. supports Hindu traditions with grants to Brahmans and restorations of major temples
    b. supports Buddhist traditions by building *viharas* and employing Buddhist priests (*vajracaryas*) at court
    c. revived festivals from earlier periods
3. Hinduism
    a. Pervasive influence of Mithila Hindu culture: Mithila Brahmans imported to serve in royal courts and temples, regarded as greater in learning than local Brahmans
    b. royal cult to Taleju, a manifestation of Durga, likely imported
    c. Brahmanical norms of caste and religious observance mediated through Mithila Brahmans
    d. continuity of ancient traditions upheld through royal patronage
    e. festival innovation: *Gai Jatra*

4. Buddhism
    a. decline in former monasteries, although the Valley remains an important repository for Indian Buddhist texts
    b. in later Malla period, Tibetan Buddhist lamas influential at key local shrines
        1. rebuilt Svayambhu and Bauddha periodically
        2. extension of teaching lineages
    c. Tibetan pilgrims regularly visit the Valley
    d. Tibetan art imported, a dominant influence on local artists

IV. Nepal in the Modern Period: 1800 AD--Present

A. Core Area: the area of conquest by the Gorkhali armies from Kathmandu
    1. Chamba in the west
    2. Sikkim in the east

B. Historical Sources
    1. Epigraphy
        a. Shah dynasty inscriptions
        b. *lal mohar* (document seals)
        c. copper plate inscriptions
    2. Numismatics: Shah coinage
    3. Art and Archaeology
        a. religious architecture
        b. royal architecture
        c. domestic architecture
        d. painting
        e. sculpture
    4. Outside Sources
        a. Indian scholarship in Nepal
            1. Bhagavanlal Indraji
            2. Rahul Sankrtyayana
        b. Tibetan archives
        c. Chinese archives
        d. English accounts
            1. Kirkpatrick
            2. Buchanan-Hamilton
            3. Hodgson
            4. Oldfield
            5. Landon
            6. documents of the Government of India
        e. other Scholars:
            1. Sylvain Levi
            2. Minayeff

3. Buhler
4. Kawakita
5. Local Sources
    a. chronicles
    b. *Dibyopadesa* of Prithvi Narayan
    c. panegyric poetry
    d. development of archives
        1. government offices
        2. family archives
        3. economic records

C. Major Events

1. Beginnings of the Gorkha state up to the Anglo-Nepali War, 1814-1816
    a. the death of Prithvi Narayan: 1775
    b. conquest to the west and east: Chamba to Bhutan
    c. Nepal-Tibet War of 1793
    d. extension of the Shah administration
    e. rivalry at the court
        1. the institution of Prime Minister
        2. Parbatiya-Newar factions

2. Anglo-Nepali War of 1814-1816
    a. the War: its causes and consequences
        1. Gorkha conquests east and western Himalayas disturb British
        2. Gorkha attacks in the plains areas make British begin military operations
    b. Treaty of Sagauli (1816): Consequences of war
        1. Nepal loses, surrenders when British enter Kathmandu Valley
        2. British reduce Nepal to present east-west borders of Mechi and Mahakali Rivers
        3. Nepal stripped of most lands in the Terai
        4. Nepalese soldiers are now enlisted in British Indian army
        5. British Residency established in Kathmandu

3. Era of weak Shah Rule (1816-1846)
    a. the rise of Bhim Sen Thapa (1806-1837)
    b. the rise of Jang Bahadur Kunwar: 1846
        1. the Kot Massacre, 1846
        2. the end of Pandey-Thapa rivalries

4. Rana Regime: First Period (1846-1885)
    a. The prime ministership of Jang Bahadur (1846- 1878)
        1. trip to England and return (1851)
        2. the Nepal-Tibet War, 1856
        3. support for the British during the Indian Mutiny

4. the Codification of the *Muluki Ain*, 1854
  b. accession and assassination of Ranodip Singh (1877-1885)
5. The Rana Regime: Second Period (1885-1950)
  a. the accession of the Shumshere Rana line
    1. Bir Shumshere (1885-1900)
    2. Deb Shumshere (1900-1901)
  b. Chandra Shumshere (1901-1928)
    1. the consolidation of Rana power
    2. emancipation of slaves
    3. British recognition of Nepalese Independence
  c. Bhim Shumshere (1928-1932)
  d. Juddha Shumshere (1932-1945)
    1. political repression
    2. activities of the Nepali Congress members
    3. Second World War
    4. abdication and retirement to Ridi
  e. Padma Shumshere (1945-1948)
    1. the end of British colonialism and its impact
  f. Mohan Shumshere (1948-50), the last Rana Prime Minister
    1. Indian Independence (1947) and its effects on Nepal
    2. the escape of King Tribhuvan to India, with assistance by Nehru
6. Social and Economic Organization under the Ranas
  a. economic policies of the Ranas
    1. extremely conservative policies create a state treasury that is also family purse
    2. no attempt to invest in industry or increase trade
    3. Ranas held immense tracts of land: Jang Bahadur alone claimed 2% of Nepal's land as his own
    4. taxation system to maximize revenue; created difficulties for subsistence farmers
  b. social policies
    1. caste and hierarchy
    2. attitudes toward religion
      a. strict Hindu orthodoxy
      b. Shiva-Pashupati: divine protector of realm
      c. discrimination against Buddhists
        1. ending of patronage
        2. seizure of monastic lands
        3. limitations placed on Buddhist movement
        4. Bhutanese lamas expelled
        5. Theravadin modernists expelled
7. The Rana Family
  a. internal structure and divisions specified privileges and succession to the throne

        b. family structure later formalized into three classes
            1. "Class A": those who can succeed to Prime Ministership
            2. "Class B": those who cannot but who are considered as
               legitimate offspring of marriages
            3. "Class C": illegitimate offspring of irregular
               relationships
        c. relations with royal family
            1. Ranas arrange close marriages between Shah family and
               their own children
            2. By 1900, high degree of inbreeding, making "Rana" vs.
               "Shah" of limited value in distinguishing lineages up to
               present
        d. the military
            1. Ranas held about every post in the command structure
            2. military office becomes hereditary
        e. relations with the British
            1. After Jang Bahadur's trip to England, relations became
               more cordial between Nepalese rulers and British
            2. Nepalese assist English during the Mutiny in the siege of
               Lucknow (1857)
    7. The Restoration of Shah Authority
        a. the return of Tribhuvan, 1951
        b. the death of King Tribhuvan and accession of Mahendra, 1955
        c. the creation of Parliamentary Democracy
            1. the Nepali Congress and other parties
            2. the first attempts
               a. the Koiralas
        d. foreign relations: Nepal in the community of nations
            1. relations with India
            2. relations with the Big Powers
        e. the restoration of autocracy, 1961
            1. "royal coup" outlaws party policies
            2. the institution of Pancayat Rule
            3. politics underground
               a. Nepali Congress
               b. Communist Party
               c. government repression
       f. The death of Mahendra (1972) and accession of Birendra (1972-)
            1. contrast between the new king and his father
            2. character and education of the new king
            3. popular expectations and the royal family

D. Language and literature in the l9th and 20th centuries
    1. Development of Khas-kura or Gorkhali into national language called
     Nepali

2. Early 19th century history of Nepali literature
   a. the Nepali Chronicles
   b. the translations of Hindu and Buddhist texts
   c. the poetry of Bhanubhakta Acharya, national poet of Nepal
      1. his *Ramayana*
      2. didactic works
   d. later literary figures
      1. Lekh Nath Paudyel
      2. Girishvallabh Joshi's *Bir Caritra*
   e. 20th century writing under the Ranas.
      1. the short story, novel, and play
         a. Bal Krishna Sama
         b. Laksmi Prasad Devkota
         c. Siddhi Charan Shrestha
      2. the newspaper: Gorkha Patra
   f. Nepali literature after 1950
      1. Major Poets
         a. Bhupi Sherchan
         b. Parijat
         c. Mohan Koirala
      2. Prose writers
         a. Parijat
         b. B.P. Koirala
         c. Shiv Kumar Rai
         d. Vijay Malla
      3. Newari Literature under the Ranas and Shahs
         a. the Buddhist Chronicles
         b. continuing traditions of oral and written redaction: illustrated scroll paintings with accompanying texts
         c. major twentieth century writers and scholars:
            1. Cittadhar "Hrdaya"
            2. Kedar Man "Byathit"
            3. Durga Lala Shrestha "Khwobilu"
            4. Yog Bir Singh
      4. Continued place of Sanskrit
      5. The fate of "tribal" languages
         a. their decline
         b. isolated efforts to preserve and develop their literary form
         c. post-panchayat ethnic identity movements

E. Art and Archaeology
   1. Development of Shah and Ranas styles of architecture
      a. Indian, British and European Models
      b. Rana palaces of Italian style

2. Decline of craftmanship among the Newars and realigning artisanship for the tourist market
   a. sculpture
   b. painting
   c. minor arts

F. Recent Events
1. Birendra agrees to a referendum on the system; political activity of the banned political parties restored, 1979
2. Referendum of 1980 narrowly confirms confidence in the Panchayat system, a victory for rightist forces under Prime Minister Surya Bahadur Thapa
3. Leaders of the democratic opposition, B.P. Koirala and Ganesh Man Singh, declare that they have no faith in the results
4. Politics of opposition: political activity again banned and leaders go underground
5. Death of B.P. Koirala, 1983
6. Popular opposition grows toward Panchayat government; bombings in Kathmandu shake government, 1984-85.
7. Ascendency of hard line rightist forces within panchayat system led by Marich Man Singh, Navaraj Subedi, Niranjan Thapa, 1986
8. Growth of political youth organizations associated with political repression and support of the panchayat system: the mandales
9. India closes border with Nepal and refuses to negotiate new trade agreements after disputes over Nepal's purchase of arms from China, 1989
10. Formation under Ganesh Man Singh and other Congress leaders of a Movement for the Restoration of Democracy. Movement unites all political parties of center and left at end of 1989.
11. "*Sat Gate*": beginning of the Movement. Call for general strikes and demonstrations. Violent suppression by government, February 1990.
12. Demonstrations spread to Terai and western Nepal; Kathmandu put under curfew after police firings throughout country, March 1990
13. Government capitulates in April. Government and panchayat dissolved. New interim government formed by leaders of the movement.
14. Krishna Prasad Bhattarai becomes Prime Minister. New government negotiates new treaty with India, April 1990. Commission drafts new constitution, Fall 1990.
15. Elections held in which Congress wins majority. New government formed under Girija Prasad Koirala. Defeat of Krishna Prasad Bhattarai, May 1991.
16. Tentative economic reforms of new government, as attempts to move to a market economy. Improved economic relations with India.
17. Deteriorating political relations with Bhutan over Bhutanese accusations of support for Nepalese separatists, 1992-3.

The Singha Durbar Palace

Recommended Readings and References

Ancient Period

Beal, Samuel, (trans.). *Si-yu-ki, Buddhist Records of the Western World.* London: Trubner and Company, 1884.

Regmi, D.R. *Inscriptions of Ancient Nepal.* New Delhi: Abhinav Publications, 1983.

Riccardi, Theodore, Jr. "The Inscriptions of King Manadeva at Changu Narayan," *Journal of the American Oriental Society* 109, 1989, 611-620

_____. "Buddhism in Ancient and Medieval Nepal," in A.K. Narain ed. *Studies in the History of Buddhism.* New Delhi, 1979, 265-281.

Roerich, G. (trans.). *Biography of Dharmasvamin.* Patna: Jayaswal Research Institute, 1959.

Slusser, Mary S. *Nepal Mandala.* Princeton University Press, 1982.

Vajracarya, Gautam. "Recently Discovered Inscriptions of Licchavi Nepal," *Kailash* 1, 117-133.

_____. "Yangala, Yambu." *Contributions to Nepalese Studies* 1, 1974, 90-98.

Witzel, Michael. "On the History and Present State of Vedic Tradition in Nepal," *Vasudha* XV, 1976, 17-39.

_____. "On the Location of the Licchavi Capital of Nepal," *Studien zur Indologie und Iranistik* 5/6, 1980, 311-337.

Wright, Daniel. *History of Nepal.* Trans. by Munshi Shew Shanker Singh and Pandit Shri Gunananda. Cambridge, 1877.

Middle Period

Brinkhaus, Horst. "The Descent of the Nepalese Malla Dynasty as Reflected by Local Chronicles," *Journal of the American Oriental Society* 111, 1991, 118-122.

Kolver, Bernhard. "Stages in the Evolution of a World Picture," *Numen* XXXII (2), 1985, 131-168.

Korn, Wolfgang. *The Traditional Architecture of the Kathmandu Valley.* Kathmandu: Ratna Pustak Bhandar, 1979.

Lewis, Todd T. and Lozang Jamspal. "Newars and Tibetans in the Kathmandu Valley: Three New Translations from Tibetan Sources," *Journal of Asian and African Studies* 36, 1988, 187-211.

Macdonald, A.W. and Stahl, Anne Vergati. *Newar Art*. Warminster: Aris and Phillips, 1979.

Petech, Luciano. *Medieval History of Nepal*. (2nd ed.) Rome, 1984.

Riccardi, Theodore, Jr. "The Edicts of Rama Shaha of Gorkha," *Kailash* 5, 1977, 29-66.

Shore, Sir John, ed.. "An Account of the Kingdom of Nepal by Father Giuseppe of the Capucian Order." *Asiatic Researches* 2, 1799: 307-322.

Stiller, Ludwig, S.J. *Prithvi Narayan in the Light of Dibyodesa*. Kathmandu, 1968.

Vajracarya, Dhanavajra. "The Development of Early and Medieval Settlements in the Kathmandu Valley," *Nepalica*. Sankt Augustin: VGH Wissenschaftsverlag, 1987, 357-364.

Modern Period

Baral, Lok Raj. *Nepal's Politics of Referendum*. New Delhi: Vikas, 1983.

Forum for the Protection of Human Rights. *Dawn of Democracy: People's Power in Nepal*. Kathmandu: Sahayogi, 1990.

Hodgson, Brian. *Essays on the Languages, Literature, and Religion of Nepal and Tibet*. New Delhi: Manjusri Publishing House, 1972.

Hofer, Andras. *The Caste Hierarchy and the State of Nepal, A Study of the Muluki Ain of 1854*. Innsbruck: Universitatsverlag Wagner, 1979.

Hutt, Michael. *Himalayan Voices*. Berkeley: University of California Press, 1991.

Lewis, Todd T. and Daya Ratna Shakya. "Contributions to the History of Nepal: Eastern Newar Diaspora Settlements," *Contributions to Nepalese Studies*, 15 (1), 1988, 25-65.

Malla, Kamal P. ed. *Nepal: Perspectives on Continuity and Change*. Kathmandu: CENAS, 1989.

Rana, Padma Jung Bahadur. *Life of Maharaja Sir Jung Bahadur Rana of Nepal*. Kathmandu: Ratna Pustak Bhandar, 1974.

King Mahendra. "Panchayat Politics 1960 Onwards," in Pashupati Shumshere, J. Rana and Kamal P. Malla, eds. *Nepal In Perspective*. Kathmandu: CEDA, Tribhuvan University, 1973.

Regmi, M.C. *Landownership in Nepal*. Berkeley: University of California Press, 1976.

_____. *Thatched Huts and Stucco Palaces: Peasants and Landlords in 19th Century Nepal*. New Delhi: Vikas, 1978.

_____. *A Study in Nepali Economic History 1768-1846*. New Delhi: Manjusri, 1971.

Rose, Leo E. *Nepal: Strategy for Survival*. Berkeley: University of California Press, 1971.

_____. *The Politics of Nepal*. Ithaca: Cornell University Press, 1976.

Rose, Leo and Margaret Fisher. *The Politics of Nepal: Persistence and Change in an Asian Monarchy*. Ithaca: Cornell University Press, 1970.

Rubin, David. *Nepali Visions, Nepali Dreams: The Poetry of Laxmiprasad Devkota*. New York: Columbia University Press, 1980.

Stiller, Ludwig, S.J. *The Silent Cry*. Kathmandu: Sahayogi, 1976.

Dzong in Bhutan

Chapter 8

THE EASTERN HIMALAYAS: ASSAM, SIKKIM, BHUTAN AND ARUNACHAL PRADESH

I. Definitions

    A. Assam
        1. Origin of term in name "*Ahom*"
        2. Greatly varied boundaries throughout its history

    B. Eastern Himalayas includes modern Sikkim, Bhutan and Arunachal Pradesh

    C. Area as a whole most difficult to define and least known within the Himalayas

    D. The area comprising parts of the modern states Bengal and Assam as well as Sikkim, Bhutan, and Arunachal Pradesh
        1. Physical Geography
            a. location
            b. size and extent
            c. area can be seen as a system of closely related ecological niches
            d. climate
                1. heavy monsoon, with seasonal flooding
                2. subtropical
                3. malarial
        2. Topography
            a. mountains and plains
                1. lowlands (Assam)
                2. middle ranges (Sikkim, Bhutan, Arunachal Pradesh)
                3. high Himalayas (Sikkim, Bhutan, Arunachal Pradesh)
            b. rivers and river valleys
                1. Brahmaputra river: the chief geographical feature of area, distinguishing Assam from other Himalayan areas
                2. Tista
                3. Karatoya
                4. Subansiri
            c. trade routes and passes
                1. northeast: Patki Himalayas, 16,000 ft.
                2. southeast: into Naga Hills, 6,000 ft.
                3. south: into Lushai Hills, 6,000 ft.

    3. Culture Areas
        a. submontane lowlands of Assam
        b. mid-montane Tibeto-Burman hills of Sikkim, Bhutan, and
           Arunachal Pradesh
    4. Political Units
        a. independent states
            1. Bhutan
                a. special relationship with India
                b. its international status
        b. states of the Indian Union
            1. Assam
                a. political divisions
                b. shifting administrative changes over the last
                   twenty years
            2. Arunachal Pradesh
                a. its creation out of NEFA
                b. special relations with Indian Government
            3. Union territory and Sikkim
                a. former status: independent kingdom
                b. relation with Indian Government
            4. Bengal
                a. Darjeeling and surrounding areas
            5. Processes of State Formation
                a. military conquest
                b. treaty
                c. colonization
                d. Hinduization
                e. language policy

E. Historical Areas
    1. Core Areas: Assam Valley has continuous history from ancient times
    2. Peripheral Areas: areas with little known ancient history, partially or
       imperfectly known medieval history
        a. Sikkim
        b. Bhutan
        c. Arunachal Pradesh

II. The Ancient History of Assam: 1000 BC--1200 AD

A. Prehistory
    1. Paleontology
        a. animal finds
        b. human remains
    2. paleolithic culture

    a. stray surface finds

    b. sites

   3. neolithic

    a. stray finds

      1. Assam

      2. Darrang

B. Historical sources

  1. Indigenous: Kamarupa and Pragjyotisha

    a. epigraphy

      1. the inscriptions of the Bhaumanarakas

      2. the Umachal Rock Incriptions of the 5th century AD

      3. the Badaganga Rock Inscription of the 6th century AD

      4. inscriptions of Bhaskaravarman of the 7th century AD

    b. numismatics: little coinage from ancient Assam

    c. art and archaeology: no major sites yet described

  2. Outside sources

    a. Indian references in epic literature: *Mahabharata* and *puranas*

    b. Tibetan Buddhist Histories

    c. Chinese Histories: "*Kia-mo-lu-po*"

    d. Classical sources

  3. Mythology: Origins, Sacred Geography, Sacred Time

    a. Sacred texts

      1. the myth of Kamakhyadevi

      2. the *Jogini Tantra*

      3. the *Kali Purana*

      4. the *natha* and *siddha* traditions

    b. The Chronicles (*buranji*)

      1. the nature and origin

        a. major *buranjis*

        b. minor *buranjis*

      2. their time frame

      3. their language

    c. the structure of sacred time and space

      1. the *yugas*

      2. Assamese sacred geography

      3. human time and sacred time

        a. the beginning of dynastic history

        b. the end of human history

C. Political History

  1. Legendary beginnings

  2. Assam before the Varmans

    a. mentioned as a source of silver

    b. old theories of Aryan, Dravidian, "primitive"

       c. late Vedic and early epic literature refers to eastern India as home of mleccha or barbarians; Brahmanas refer to settlements on the Karatoya

       d. by 100 AD high likelihood of Aryan speakers settling in the Brahmaputra Valley

   3. The Varman Era (ca. 280-660 AD)

       a. early kingdom with its legendary capital at Kamarupa

       b. ruling lineage traces origins to Bhagadatta, son of demon Naraka, son of Vishnu as boar *avatara*, and an earth goddess

       c. at height of Gupta empire, Kamarupa a distant tributary; once the center declined, Varmans controlled land further west

       d. Gupta Allahabad pillar mentions Kamarupa as "*pratyanta*", or frontier province

       e. Bhaskaravarman (ca. 580-648 AD)

          1. the most famous of the dynasty, performed the asvamedha, the Vedic horse sacrifice

          2. invited the Chinese pilgrim Hsuan Tsang to Assam and then accompanied him to visit King Harsha of Kanauj in 644 AD

          3. supported Chinese-led retaliation against Harsa's usurper with Nepalese and Tibetans

          4. fond of learning, a great patron of culture, especially land grants to Brahmans

          5. royal tiles of *maharajadhiraja* and *paramabhattaraka*

       f. King Salastambha (7th century)

       g. Pralamba era (8th-9th century)

   4. the Palas of Bengal

       a. influence in the eastern hills and in Assam

       b. major rulers and centers of power

D. Social and Economic Organization

   1. tribal peoples, practicing subsistence agriculture in interaction with Aryan-speaking peoples who introduce intensive wet-rice cultivation

   2. much of the tribal mountain areas remain unaffected by plains culture of India

   3. society monarchical, with Indicized elite ruling non-Aryan speaking tribal agricultural populations

E. Relations with Adjacent Areas

   1. although little documentation of relations with Tibet or other regions exist, contact seems likely

   2. little evidence to support assertions that Bhutan, Sikkim, or Arunachal Pradesh formed part of Kamarupa in this era

F. Religion
1. *Naga* worship mentioned in the earliest records
2. Worship of *devi* gave Assam a distinctive Hindu identity
    a. centered at the Kamakhya *pitha*
    b. site known throughout India in the ancient period
3. Related to this, Assam is associated with the rise of tantra and the practices of the *siddhas*

G. Language and Literature
1. Eastern *prakrits*
2. Important tantric literature in Sanskrit
    a. *Jogini Tantra*
    b. *Hevajra Tantra*
    c. the texts of the *nathas* and *siddhas*

III. The Ancient History of the Eastern Himalayas: Sikkim, Bhutan, and Arunchal Pradesh (1000 BC-1000 AD)

A. Definition
1. Periphery of the ancient period
2. Little textual or archaeological evidence: the names Bhutan, Sikkim, and "Arunachal Pradesh" all later in origin

B. Prehistory
1. Paleontology
    a. animal finds
    b. human remains
2. Paleolithic culture
    a. stray surface finds
    b. sites
3. Neolithic stray finds
    a. Sikkim
    b. Bhutan
    c. Arunachal Pradesh

C. Bhutan
1. Periphery of Tibet
2. Temple construction of Srong Btsan-sGampo (c. 627- 649 AD)
    a. temple of Paro
    b. Bum-thang

D. The earliest history of Sikkim: Lepcha folklore

E. Language and Literature
 1. Sanskrit
 2. Tibetan
 3. Development of Assamese and other vernaculars
 4. Tribal languages

IV. The History of Assam in the Middle Period: 1200--1800 AD

A. Definition of Core Area and other regions: the civilization centered in the Brahmaputra River Valley, i.e. Kamarupa/Assam

B. Historical Sources
 1. Epigraphy
 2. Numismatics
 3. Art and archaeology
    a. paucity and fragmented nature of sources
    b. Shivasagar: site of important illustrated manuscripts and wood carving
    c. lack of monuments and other physical remains due to floods and earthquakes
 4. Outside sources
    a. Indian
    b. Tibetan
    c. Chinese

C. Political History of Kamarupa/Assam in the Ahom Period (1200-1826 AD)
 1. Area dominated by migrations of tribes from Upper Burma, a branch of the Shan
 2. *Kshatriya* castes called *bhuyans* expanded areas of state control up the Brahmaputra and major tributaries that were suitable for wet-rice cultivation
 3. Mughul invasions ordered by Aurungzeb under Mir Jumla, ended in disaster for the invaders: Assamese retreat practicing scorched earth policy and finally rout imperial army
 4. Other Muslim invasions end in same result and Assam acquires a dreadful reputation at Mughul court
 5. Western towns fortified as result of subsequent threats: Gauhati, Hajo
 6. Dominance of Tungkhungia Ahoms (1681-1826)
    a. era when famine reduces population by thirty percent
 7. Rivalry of *bhuyans* and Ahom elite
 8. Growth of Vaishnavism

D. Social, Political and Economic Organization
1. Ahoms using plough, wet rice agriculture that relied on water buffalo
2. Ahoms become dominant elite with own religion
3. Ahom political organization
   a. based on extensive irrigation system that relied on forced labor
   b. key alliances between rulers and *bhuyans*
   c. male population (ages 15-60) organized militia; one fourth worked on expanding irrigation
   d. militia helped subdue tribal people of upper Assam, converting their subsistence from slash and burn agriculture (*jhum*) to intensive wet rice cultivation
   e. *brahmans* received land grants in return for organizing frontier settlement
4. Importance of the slavery
   a. estimated at 5-10 percent of the population
   b. nature of slavery not yet known
5. The Militia
   a. organized male groups into *paiks*, each of which was composed of several cells called *gots*
   b. *paiks* held common rice land and also areas in which they had exclusive forest use, as well as grazing and fishing rights
   c. individuals got 2-4 acres of land in return for working state land
6. Social classes
   a. caste categories adopted by many groups in Assam, but there are few instances of *jajmani* relations
      1. Ahoms
      2. *bhuyans*
      3. upper castes: *brahmans*, *kayasthas*
      4. predominant agricultural caste: *kalitas*
      5. artisan castes
      6. low castes: *dhobi*, *chandela*
   b. tribal society had marginal connections to central society; many groups remained independent well into the twentieth century
   c. Vaishnava monasteries called *satras*
      1. by 1600, widescale importance in colonizing frontier territories, obtaining slaves, establishing land grants
      2. used as refuges from political exploitation: connection between peasant uprisings and spread of *satras*
7. Trade
   a. local products: elephants, ivory, knives, gold incense, iron
   b. paucity of raw materials
   c. small surplus in circulation

        d. trade relations with outside areas
              1. entrepot between Bengal and Inner Asia
              2. trade with Tibet in horses: salt, wool, musk, from the Tibetan areas in exchange for rice, spices, iron

V. History of the Eastern Himalayas in the Middle Period: 1200--1800 AD

A. Bhutan

1. By 12th century, small principalities ruled by theocratic governments in control of powerful Tibetan families
2. Cultural and political ties to Tibet are very close
3. Political power in Bhutan: the Drukpa sect
    a. history of Drukpa sect
        1. its leader in Bhutan, Ngawang Namgyal
            a. first Dharmaraja of Bhutan
            b. his political career
        2. political and religious insititutions
            a. established by Namgyal
            b. last until 1907
    b. Bhutan remains isolated from Ahoms and Mughuls
    c. Differences between Bhutanese and Tibetan culture and society
4. Bhutan and the East India Company
    a. Bhutan's commercial ties with Bengal and Assam
    b. raids of Bhutanese on Cooch Behar
    c. conflict with the Assamese and British
    d. Warren Hastings and Bhutan

B. Sikkim

1. Legendary accounts of kings of Tibetan and Indian origin
2. Phun-tsho-Namgyal, first king of Sikkim (1604-AD)
3. Invasion by Bhutan, 1700
4. Invasion by Nepal
    a. the attacks by Jor Singh
    b. invasion led by Damodar Pande
    c. the Sino-Nepalese War of 1793 and its effects

VI. Assam & the Eastern Himalayas in the Modern Period: 1800 AD--Present

A. Core Areas: Assam, Bhutan, Sikkim, Arunachal Pradesh (NEFA)
    1. Historical Sources
        a. epigraphy
        b. numismatics
        c. art and archaeology: modern monuments and sites
    2. Indigenous Sources
        a. printed sources
        b. government archives
        c. royal and religious architecture
        d. public architecture
    3. Outside Sources
        a. Indian government archives
        b. Tibetan archives
        c. sources and accounts in English
            1. Gait
            2. Bogle
            3. Turner
            4. Eden
            5. Markham
            6. Bhuyan

B. Assam: Major Events and Themes
    1. The decline of Ahom power
        a. internal dissension
        b. friction with *bar phukan*
        c. appeals to British by Gaurinath Singh, 1786
        d. Burmese invade Assam in 1817 at request of the *bar phukan*, Badan Chanda
        e. British drive out Burmese: Treaty of Yangdabo, 1826
    2. Assam assimilated into Bengal, 1905
        a. separate province of Assam created in 1877 amalgamated with Bengal in 1905
        b. separated in 1924, it remained distinct through Independence to the present day
        c. Japanese incursions into Assam during the Second World War
    3. Creation of separate states: Nagaland, Meghalaya, United Khasi and Jantia Hills District, Union Territory of Mizoram
    4. NEFA becomes Arunachal Pradesh, 1962
    5. Naga hills district created, 1963

6. Meghalaya created from Garo district and United Khasi and Jaintia Hills District, 1970
7. Union Territory of Mizoram created, 1972
8. Union Territory of Arunachal Pradesh created, 1972
9. Journalists and westerners barred from Assam, 1975-
10. Deportation agitations against Bengaladesh refugees begin, 1985
11. Arunachal achieves statehood, 1987 with capital at Itanagar
12. Pragjyotisapura, near Gauhati, designated as new capital of Assam, 1987
13. Bodos agitate for separate state, 1989-90 in area between Assam and Bengaladesh
14. Tourist groups permitted, 1994

C. Bhutan: Major Events and Themes

1. Separate religious and secular authorities replaced by monarchy, 1907
2. British take passes to Darrang, 1841
3. Eden Mission, 1863
4. British invasion of Bhutan, 1865; Treaty of Sinchula: Athara and other passes ceded to British
5. Bhutanese accept guidance of British in foreign affairs, 1910, amid Chinese protests
6. Treaty with India, 1949, continuing former relationship with British with independent India
7. Chinese invasion of Tibet in 1949 creates refugee problem for Bhutan; total number refugees estimated at 8,000, only 3,000 of which accept citizenship
8. Nepalese immigrant population increases so that they gradually form majority of the population
9. King Dorji Wangchuk dies; Succeeded by Jigme Singye Wangchuk, 1972
10. Government continues policy of restricted visa for foreign tourists in order to preserve "cultural purity"
11. Bhutanese government pursues more aggressive policy with regard to independence from India despite its heavy dependence on Indian economic aid
12. Prince Jigme Gesar Wangyal Wangchuk designated heir to the throne, 1989
13. Expulsion of 9,000 non-Drukpas, 1989
14. Government alarmed by the restoration of democracy in Nepal; even stricter policy of cultural isolation and purity; foreign TV programs banned. TV dishes ordered dismantled. Strict enforcement of Driglam Manzha, edicts referring to dress and conduct. Demonstrations by Peoples' Forum for Human Rights.
15. Bhutanese living in Nepal demonstrate on border and in Kathmandu, 1990

16. Pro-democracy agitations continue, 1991-2; Dissatisfaction among Bhutanese of Nepalese origin grows; Bhutan People's Party charges government with attacks and arrests of Nepalese; leaders defect to Nepal and form "liberation" organization.
17. 80,000 refugees flee Bhutan for India and Nepal
18. Protracted, inconclusive negotiations between Nepal and Bhutan fail to resolve dispute, 1993-4

D. Sikkim and Darjeeling: Major Events and Themes
1. the Anglo-Nepalese Treaty of 1814-16 and its effects
2. Darjeeling ceded to British by Sikkim, 1839
3. the capture of Hooker and Campbell, 1849
4. the British expedition of 1850
    a. annexation of Sikkim Tarai by the British
    b. the Anglo-Sikkimese Treaty of March, 1861
5. status of Sikkim at Indian Independence
6. political movements within Sikkim
    a. the Chogyal and his party
    b. Nepali immigrants as political force
    c. actions of Indian Government in Sikkim
7. Creation of Union Territory of Sikkim.
8. Political reforms demanded by National Congress and Janata Congress; at request of Chogyal, Indian police invited to maintain order, 1973.
9. Elections for popular elected assembly; Samgram Parishad party wins majority; Government of Sikkim Act; Chogyal becomes constitutional monarch under Constitution Act, 1974. Sikkim becomes a state associated with Indian Union, 1975.
10. Chogyal deposed and office abolished; Constitution Act makes Sikkim 22nd state of the Indian Union, 1975
11. Chogyal dies in America, 1982
12. Elections held; Sangram Parishad Government continues in power; Chief Minister: Nara Bahadur Bhandari, 1989.
13. Events in Darjeeling, 1979-1995
    a. Indian Prime Minister Morarji Desai claims that Nepali is a language of foreigners, 1979.
    b. Call by Subhas B. Ghising for a separate homeland to be called Gorkhaland. Formation of the Gorkha National Liberation Front. Bengal Chief Minister Jyoti Basu declares movement anti-national.
    c. Gorkha separatists campaign for Gorkhaland through strikes and terrorist action. Agreement signed with Indian government creating a Darjeeling Gorkha Hill Council with limited autonomy, 1988.
    d. End of successionist movement; slow return of hill station economy.

E. Social and Economic Organization under the British
1. Assam
 a. imperial economic policies
  1. land
  2. taxation
  3. trade
   a. introduction of tea and chinchona
   b. management of plantations
  4. migrant labor
 b. social change
  1. caste and tribe
  2. attitudes towards Hinduism
  3. admission of Christian missionaries
  4. British life in Assam
  5. effects of migrant communities: Bangladeshi, Nepali
2. Bhutan and Sikkim
 a. imperial economic policies
  1. trade policies
  2. land and taxation policies
  3. Darjeeling: economy of a hill station
 b. social change
  1. effects of newly established monarchy in Bhutan
  2. relations between monastery and lay population
  3. Lepcha and other tribal populations marginalized in new state
  4. Nepalese immigration

F. Economic and Social Organization after Independence
1. Assam
 a. economic development
  1. new Indian government policies
  2. planning and its effects
  3. chief industries
   a. mining
   b. oil
   c. tea
 b. social organization and change
  1. effects of continued migration
  2. population growth
2. Bhutan
 a. economic development
  1. heavy reliance on Indian aid which is forty per-cent of all outside aid
  2. new emphasis on education

3. growing timber industry
4. southern city of Phuntsoling becomes major commercial center.
    b. social organization and change
        1. continued growth of Nepalese population leads to political and social tension
        2. new social policies of government designed to preserve Druk-pa power
        3. Sikkim
            a. economic development
                1. massive Indian aid to Sikkim
                2. new emphasis on education
            b. social organization and change
                1. continued growth of Nepalese population
                2. assimilation of Sikkim into the Indian Union

G. Language and Literature in the 19th and 20th centuries

1. The growth of the Assamese language
    a. relation to Bengali and Oriya
    b. the rise of modern literature
    c. influence of modern Bengali literature
    d. influence of English language and literature
2. Language in Bhutan and Sikkim
    a. the growth of national languages
    b. Nepali as a lingua franca and its influence
    c. the position of English
    d. the tribal languages
        1. Lepcha in Sikkim
        2. Limbu in Sikkim
        3. the tribal languages of Bhutan
        4. the tribal languages of Arunachal Pradesh

Recommended Readings and References

Ancient Period

Gait, Edward. *A History of Assam*. Calcutta: Thacker, Spink and Company 1906.

Siiger, Halfdan. *Ethnological Field-Research in Chitral, Sikkim, and Assam: A Preliminary Report*. Historik-fiiogogiske Videnskabernes Selskab, Bind 36 (2), 1956.

Sharma, Tarun C. "Prehistoric Archaeology in North Eastern India--A Review of Progress," in T.C. Sharma and D.N. Majumdar, eds. *Eastern Himalayas: A Study of Anthropology and Tribalism*. New Delhi: Cosmo Publications, 1977.

Middle Period

Aris, Michael. *Bhutan*. New Delhi: Vikas, 1980.

Bhuyan, S.K. *Atan Buragohain and his Times*. Gauhati: Lawyers Book Stall, 1957.

Bhuyan, S.K. *A History of Assam*. London: Oxford University Press, 1933.

Guha, Amalendu. "The Medieval Economy of Assam," in *Cambridge History of India*. Vol. II, 1982.

Risley, H.H. "History of Sikkim and its Rulers," *Gazeteer of Sikkim*. New Delhi: Manjusri Press, 1972.

Modern Period

Hazarika, Sanjoy. *Strangers of the Mist: Tales of War and Peace from India's Northeast*. New Delhi : Penguin India, 1994.

Markham, Clement (ed.) *Narratives of the Mission of George Bogle to Tibet, and of the Journey of Thomas Manning to Lhasa*. New Delhi: Manjusri, 1971.

Prabhakara, M.S. "Together and Apart: Stir for an Autonomous State in Assam," *Frontline* 10/31/1987, 30-41.

Rose, Leo. *The Politics of Bhutan*. Ithaca: Cornell University Press, 1977.

Turner, Samuel. *An Account of An Embassy to the Court of the Teshoo Lama, in Tibet, Containing a Narration of a Journey Through Bootan, and Part of Tibet.* New Delhi: Manjusri Publishing House, Bibliotheca Himalayica, Series 1, Vol. 4, 1971. (Reprint)

Younghusband, Sir Francis. *India and Tibet.* New Delhi: Oriental Publishers, 1971.

Weiner, Myron. "The Political Demography of Assam's Anti-Immigrant Movement," *Population and Development Review* 9 (2), 1983, 279-292.

Settlement in Bhutan

Early Shah Ruler of Nepal

Chapter 9

THE EFFECTS OF MODERN STATE FORMATION ON THE HIMALAYAN PEOPLE

I. Introduction

A. Small political-territorial units provide the chief organizing principle for regional life before modern states emerge

B. Territorially-nucleated stratified lineages belonging to a locally dominant caste commonly control these regions and states

C. The modern state boundaries imposed across the Himalayan landscape are often at odds with the logic of ethnic and linguistic divisions

D. Submission to the laws of the different states now controlling the region -- economic systems (banking, development projects), educational institutions, police and judicial authorities -- has affected the peoples of each region differently

II. Nepal: The Rule of Gorkha (1769-present)

A. Modern Nepal has exerted a formative influence in the Himalayan region, extending a distinctive variation of Hindu rule across the state's domain

B. Ethnic groups dealt with Shah military ambitions in different ways:
   1. Peoples of the central hills -- Gurungs and Magars -- worked as mercenaries in the Gorkha armies
   2. Newars in the Kathmandu Valley after conquest set up production and supply networks throughout the Himalayan region
   3. Peoples of the eastern hills were conquered militarily and then integrated under state rule by their chiefs assuming revenue-gathering positions

C. Gorkhalis utilized slavery as an instrument of conquest
  1. Tax debtors
  2. Tibetanized peoples or tribals who slaughtered cows could be enslaved according to the *Muluki Ain*

D. The Spread of cultural practices favored by the Shahs
  1. Ruling elite saw nation as "*Asal Hindusthan*" ("A true Hindu kingdom") and sought to apply this ideal in every domain of life
  2. Shahs lavish patrons of the Gorakhnath sect and Hindu festivals
  3. *Dasain*: National Festival
      a. festival dedicated to the worship the goddess Durga in the autumn
      b. Underlying the religious dimensions is an element of nationalism:
          1. until the 1950s, every village headmen and tribal leader throughout Nepal had to supply the local Gorkhali militia with animals for sacrifice
          2. these animals, in turn, were sacrificed to the goddess in the name of the king and on behalf of his rule
      c. The name of the king is invoked in the traditional *Dasain* blessing given by every clan elder to his junior kinsmen at the climax of the festival
      d. the celebration of *Dasain* can be seen as an affirmation of "cultural loyalty" to the kingdom of Nepal

E. The Imposition of Gorkhali law: the *Muluki Ain*
  1. Promulgated in Nepal during the reign of the first Rana Prime Minister, Jung Bahadur Rana, 1853
  2. Each apparently discrete ethnic population was defined as a *jat* -- a term roughly equivalent to the Sanskrit *jati* meaning race, lineage, tribe, or, more colloquially, caste -- for the purpose of ranking within the legal code hierarchy
  3. The place of any particular group within the social hierarchy outlined in the *Muluki Ain* was contrived on the basis of the existing knowledge of that group which was often incomplete
  4. Hierarchy:
      a. gave preeminence to the "twice born" or ritually pure groups (*tagadhari*), primarily *brahmans* and *kshatriyas* (Nep.: *chetri*)
      b. ranked beneath the *tagadhari* in the ritual hierarchy were the *matwali*, or "liquor drinking" *jat*, a category that included most of the Tibeto-Burman hill populations.
      c. ranked beneath the matwali were the artisan and menial groups, or *pani nacalnya* (lit., "from whom [others] accept no water"),

who are considered impure owing to some ritually defiling aspect of their traditional occupations.

    d. *pani nachalnya* divided into two divisions, the second corresponding to the true untouchables:

       1. *namasinya* ("non-enslavable")

       2. *masinya* ("enslavable")

5. *Muluki Ain* system implemented by administration of regional governors (*subbas*) and village revenue representatives (*mukhiyas*)

6. Slavery officially ended in 1924; corvee labor ended in 1951

F. Hindu rule was often anti-Muslim and anti-Buddhist

    1. *Muluki Ain* prescribed penalties for any "cow-killers" so that all yak-eating groups as well were subject to punishments including enslavement

    2. Little attempt to patronize Buddhist religious institutions

    3. Land reform actions often directed against Buddhist land endowments

III. The Indian Himalayan States: Kashmir, Himachal Pradesh, Uttar Pradesh, Sikkim, Arunachal Pradesh

A. Advantages of being part of the British empire to 1947:

    1. Access to transportation, centers of industrial development;

    2. Awareness of modern trends in every field, intellectually, technologically, in business, etc.

    3. Extension of governmental services

    4. Educational opportunities

    5. In many places, British rule broke down the magnitude of high caste dominance, creating opportunities for lower castes

B. Negative Effects of British and Indian national rule

    1. State lines established by colonial government were often ill-conceived and bequeathed myriad problems

    2. Pattern of plains centers of economic and political power practicing "internal colonialism" when relating to the mountainous regions

       a. environmental degradation

          1. logging forests for railroad construction

          2. strip-mining

          3. tea, cardamon plantation economies

       b. creating political entities that limit the ability of hill peoples to have an adequate voice in their own regional affairs

       c. in the northeast, little early concern with bringing the peoples into the nation; rapid integration over the past few decades, especially via mass in- migration, being fiercely resisted by indigenous peoples

IV. Bhutan

    A. Since state formation in seventeenth century, relationship with Lhasa oscillates between alliance and periods of hostility

    B. Peculiar relationship with the Indian government
        1. Foreign affairs in consultation with India
        2. Dependence on Indian economical aid
        3. Attempts to preserve its own distinct culture

V. Direct Chinese Rule and the End of Autonomous Tibet

    A. Chinese persecution of monastic institutions and the flight of the Dalai Lama in 1959

    B. Red Guard cadres during the Cultural Revolution (1966-1976) raze many monasteries throughout Tibet

    C. In the 1980's, evidence of greater religious freedom and of local communities rebuilding local monasteries in Chinese territory

    D. Effects in the Himalayan regions
        1. Uprooted the web of Tibetan monasticism that extended across the highlands
        2. Centers and states on the former periphery became the only societies where traditional Tibetan polities endured
        3. Disrupted the trade networks that crossed the Himalayan frontier and undermined the subsistence strategies that supported upland peoples on both sides of the border

    E. These effects accentuated the transformation of many Tibeto-Burman peoples into the modern Nepalese and Indian societies and toward more Hinduized lifestyles

Recommended Readings and References

Avedon, John. *In Exile from the Land of Snows*. New York: Vintage, 1984.

Burghart, Richard. "The Formation of the Concept of Nation-State in Nepal," *Journal of Asian Studies*, 44, 1984, 101-125.

Embree, Ainslie T. "Frontiers into Boundaries: From the Traditional to the Modern State," in Richard G. Fox ed. *Realm and Region in Traditional India*. Duke University Press, 1977, 255-280.

English, Richard. "Himalayan State Formation and the Impact of British Rule in the Nineteenth Century," *Mountain Research and Development* 5 (1), 1985, 61-78.

Goldstein, Melvyn C. *A History of Modern Tibet, 1913-1951: The Demise of the Lamaist State*. Berkeley: University of California Press, 1989.

_____. "The Dragon and the Snow Lion: The Tibet Question in the 20th Century," *Tibetan Review* XXVI (4), April 1991, 9-26.

Hopkirk, Peter. *Tresspassers on the Roof of the World*. Los Angeles: Jeremy Tarcher, 1990.

Ispahani, Mahnaz Z. *Roads and Rivals*: *The Political Uses of Access in the Borderlands of Asia*. Ithaca: Cornell University Press, 1989.

Karan, Pradyumna P. *The Himalayan Kingdoms: Bhutan, Sikkim, Nepal*. London: Van Nostrand, 1963.

_____. *The Changing Face of Tibet: Effects of Chinese Rule*. Lexington: The University Press of Kentucky, 1976.

Levine, Nancy. "Caste, State, and Ethnic Boundaries in Nepal," *Journal of Asian Studies* 46 (1), 1987, 71-88.

Mahapatra, L.K. "Pastoralists and the Modern Indian State," in Lawrence Leshnik and Gunther-Dietz Sonheimer eds. *Pastoralists and Nomads in South Asia*. Wisebaden: Otto Harrassowitz, 1975, 209-219.

Malla, Kamal P. *The Road to Nowhere*. Kathmandu: Sajha Prakashan, 1979.

Nyman, Lars-Erik. "Tawang-- A Case Study of British Frontier Policy in the Himalayas," *Journal of Asian History* 10, 1976, 151-171.

Regmi, Mahesh Chandra. *Landownership in Nepal*. Berkeley: University of California Press, 1976.

_____. *Thatched Huts and Stucco Palaces*. New Delhi: Vikas, 1978.

Rose, Leo E. "The Secularization of a Hindu Polity: The Case of Nepal," in Donald E. Smith ed. *Religion and Political Modernization*. New Haven: Yale University Press, 1974, 31-48.

_____. "Sino-Tibetan Rivalry and the Himalayan Border States," *Orbis* 5, 1961-2, 198-215.

Stiller, Ludwig F., S.J. *The Rise of the House of Gorkha*. Ranchi: The Catholic Press, 1973.

_____. *Nepal : The Growth of a Nation*. Kathmandu, Human Resources Development Research Center, 1993.

Subba, Tanka B. *Ethnicity, State and Development: A Case of the Gorkhaland Movement in Darjeeling*. New Delhi: Vikas, 1992.

Tucker, Richard P. "The Evolution of Transhumant Grazing in the Punjab Himalaya," *Mountain Research and Development* 6 (1), 1986, 17-28.

_____. "The British Colonial System and the Forests of the Western Himalaya, 1815-1914," in Richard Tucker and J.F. Richards, eds. *Global Deforestation and the 19th Century World Economy*. Durham: Duke University Press, 1983.

Uprety, Prem R. *Nepal-Tibet Relations, 1850-1930*. Kathmandu: Puja Nara, 1980.

Weiner, Myron. "The Political Demography of Nepal," *Asian Survey* 12, 1973, 617-630.

PART III:

FOUR ETHNO-GEOGRAPHIC REGIONS

6

Six Ethnographic Regions

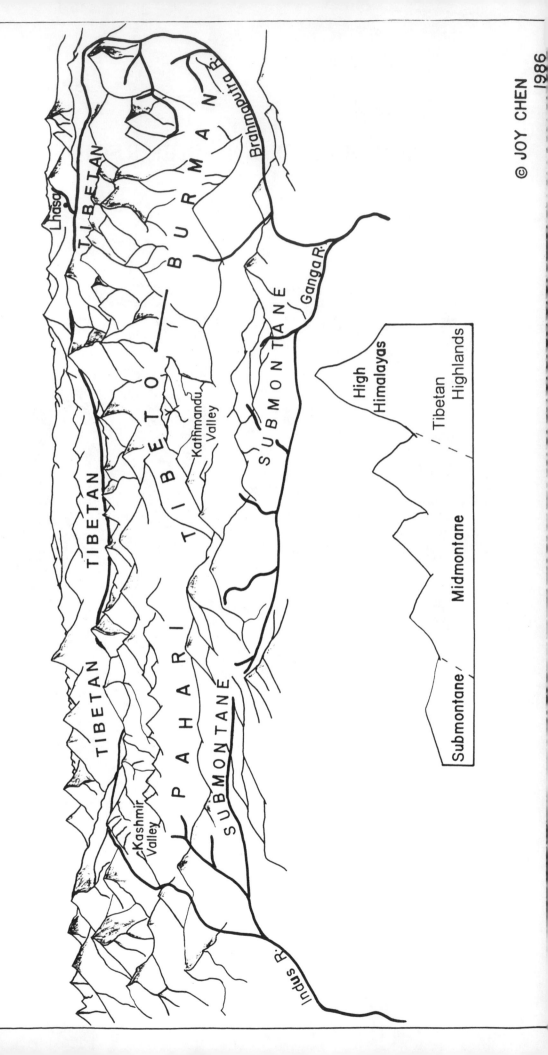

© JOY CHEN 1986

Lhasa

TIBETAN

BURMAN

Brahmaputra R.

TIBETO

Ganga R.

Kathmandu Valley

SUBMONTANE

TIBETAN

PAHARI

Kashmir Valley

SUBMONTANE

Indus R.

High Himalayas

Tibetan Highlands

Midmontane

Submontane

Chapter 10

THE SUBMONTANE REGION

I. Physical Geography

    A. Map Location: Lowlands below 2,500 ft. from Himachal Pradesh east to Arunachal Pradesh

    B. Topography
       1. Terms
          a. "*Terai*", term used in western and Nepalese regions
          b. "*Duar*", term used in the eastern region
          c. in some areas, the first low mountain range, the Shivalekhs (also called the Churia Hills in Nepal) has created small valleys called *duns*; in the submontane, these are called the "inner Terai"
          d. includes mountains on the southern side of the Brahmaputra River
       2. Watersheds:
          a. Indus tributaries (Himachal Pradesh):
             1. Ravi
             2. Beas
          b. Ganges Tributaries:
             1. Uttar Pradesh: Yamuna, Ganga
             2. Nepal: Kali, Karnali, Rapti, Gandaki, Kosi
             3. Sikkim: Tista
          c. Brahmaputra Tributaries:
             1. Bhutan: Raidak, Manas
             2. Arunachal: Subansir, Dibang, Luhit
          d. rivers very volatile, constantly shifting their courses, causing the continual dislocation of human settlements
       3. Alluvial soil abundant

    C. Climate
       1. Rainfall decreases from east to west
       2. Extreme hot in summer season
       3. Monsoon flooding common in many places
       4. Virulent malaria in some areas checked population expansion

D. Flora & fauna
  1. Some jungle areas represent the early forest of the Indian subcontinent
  2. Animals: wild elephants, rhinoceros, tiger, *gaur*, sloth bears, *gharial*, *maggar*, deer species
  3. Rich ecosystem varies between tropical forest and tall grasslands

E. Communication networks
  1. Major river valleys provide access to inner hills, subject to seasonal passability
  2. East-west travel via mid-montane points generally takes place in lowland India; recent road construction in Nepal has cut down on this pattern
  3. Indian railroads important in many areas, especially prominent in Assam

Bhote Fishermen, Nepalese Terai

II. Subsistence and Trade Patterns

  A. Hunter-gatherers, especially fishermen, survive in remote places

  B. Shifting cultivators practice slash and burn agriculture (*jhum*) in scattered localities, mostly in the eastern region

  C. Agricultural production
    1. Rich alluvial soils and the recent eradication of malaria have supported permanent agricultural production, especially commercial cash crop agriculture
        a. rice
        b. jute
        c. sugarcane
        d. oilseeds
        e. tobacco
    2. Some parts of the region are net exporters of foodstuffs

  D. Animal husbandry
    1. Cattle and water buffalo (*bos gauris*) essential to the ecological system
    2. *Mithan* buffaloes of eastern Assam region
        a. important unit of trade and exchange
        b. not used for plowing, traction
        c. kept by free pasturing in forests; owners locate them and keep them by feeding them salt
        d. meat consumed by sacrificial cults

  E. Trade
    1. All north-south roads now have stopping points in the Terai region
    2. Retail trade controlled largely by Indians
    3. Trade networks organized by central marketplace towns
    4. For most villagers local patterns of exchange predominate

  F. Wage labor & migration
    1. Terai tribals and recent migrants form a pool of poor, often landless, agricultural labor
    2. Remittance economy is often a critical resource for continual homestead subsistence

III. Settlement Patterns

  A. Historical background
    1. Until modern times, sparsely scattered residents who developed resistance to malaria

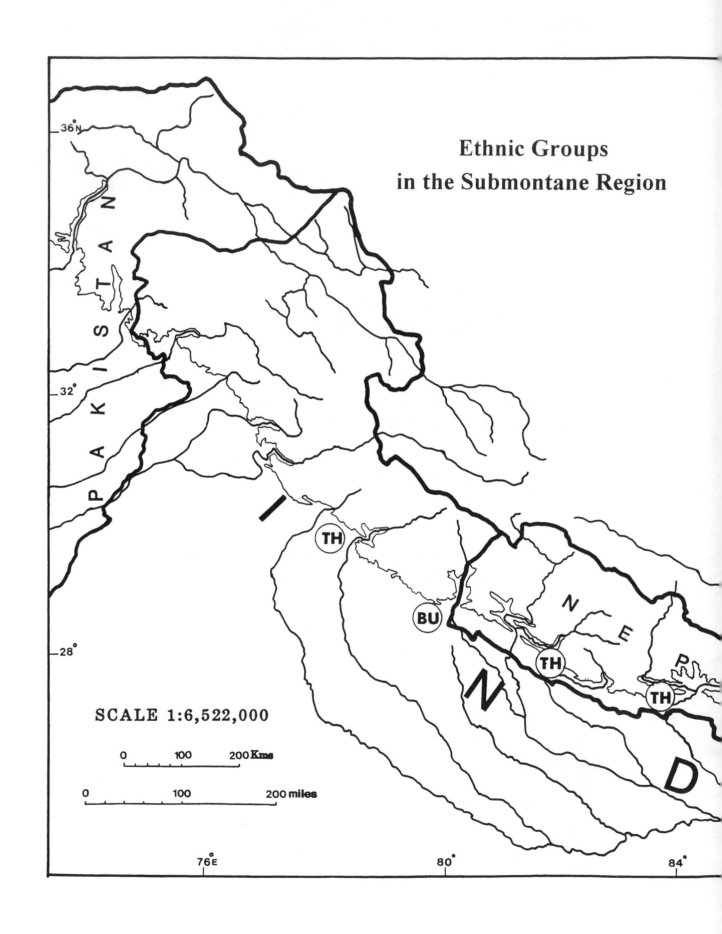

**Ethnic Groups
in the Submontane Region**

SCALE 1:6,522,000

0   100   200 Kms

0   100   200 miles

36°N

32°

28°

76°E   80°   84°

PAKISTAN

I

TH

BU

TH

TH

N

N E P

D

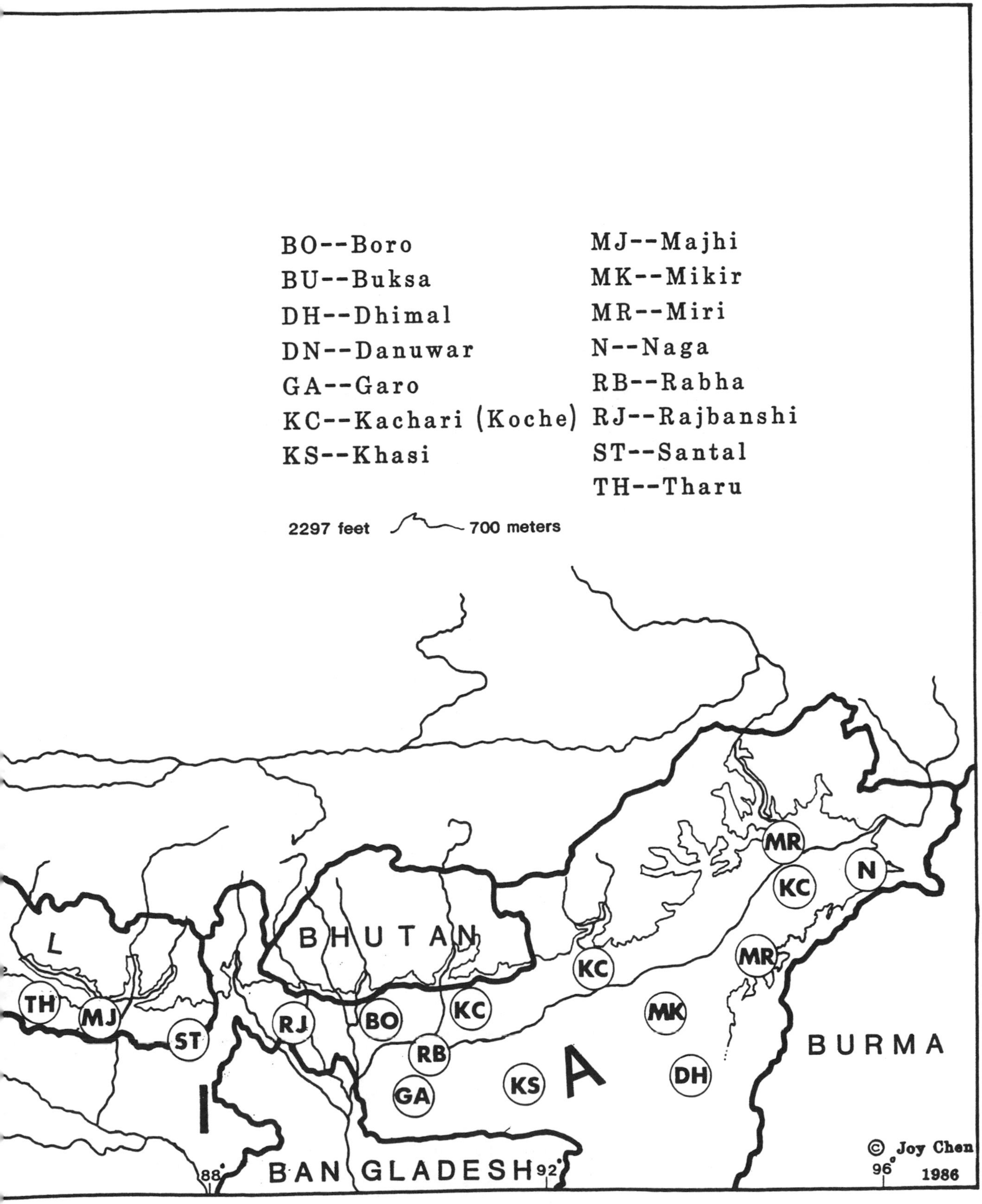

BO--Boro
BU--Buksa
DH--Dhimal
DN--Danuwar
GA--Garo
KC--Kachari (Koche)
KS--Khasi

MJ--Majhi
MK--Mikir
MR--Miri
N--Naga
RB--Rabha
RJ--Rajbanshi
ST--Santal
TH--Tharu

2297 feet ⌃‾‾ 700 meters

L

BHUTAN

TH MJ

ST

RJ BO KC

RB

GA KS

I

A

MR

KC N

MR

MK

DH

BURMA

© Joy Chen
1986

88 BANGLADESH 92 96

2. Ancient cities known in Indic literatures
    a. Lumbini, birthplace of the Buddha
    b. Kapilavastu, the Buddha's father's capital city
    c. Janakpur, associated with the Ramayana
    d. Kamakhya, an early site associated with tantric traditions
3. Late middle period: proliferation of Hindu states:
    a. Dehra Dun (Uttar Pradesh)
    b. Makwanpur (Nepal)
    c. Vijayapur (Bihar)
    d. Koch Behar (West Bengal)
4. Tea plantations and timber cutting drew peoples from across the region into the British submontane areas
5. British encouragement of Nepali herders settling lowlands of Sikkim & Assam
6. Nepali settlement in the northeast Himalayas a result of Shah state policies
7. Ongoing large-scale migration from the hills making strong impact on lowland economies

B. Village settlements
    1. Shifting rivers cause settlement shifts
    2. Characteristics vary according to ethnic groups
        a. hunter-gatherer/swidden cultivators
            1. temporary bamboo, reed, and thatched home construction
            2. small and hamleted
        b. Tharu
            1. mud walls, thatched roofs, almost windowless construction
            2. hamleted
        c. mid-hill Nepali immigrants bring mid-hill patterns of layout and house styles
        d. multi-ethnic/multi-caste character of new Nepali settlements

C. Political and commercial centers
    1. Some submontane towns began as markets and/or custom posts created by the Gorkha State or by the British Raj to stimulate commerce and derive revenue
    2. Major towns: centers for merchants, bureaucrats, and laborers
        a. Jammu, center of Dogra rule and home of the maharaja of Jamma and Kashmir
        b. Dehra Dun (Uttar Pradesh), industrial and mining town in an upland valley
        c. Kotdwara and Ramnagar (Uttar Pradesh), Indian railhead and market towns
        d. Dhangadhi (Nepal), dominant city in the western Nepalese Terai
        e. Surkhet (Nepal), inner Terai gateway town to Karnali region

f. Nepalganj, transport and market town established by the Ranas in 1863
g. Bhairahava, border town close to Lumbini
h. Butwal, an emerging industrial center
i. Bharatpur, gateway community near the confluence of the Trisuli and Gandaki rivers
j. Birganj, Nepalese town adjacent to the Indian railhead town, Raxaul
k. Biratnagar, a jute and industrial center of the eastern Nepalese Terai
l. Dharan, a gateway town north of Biratnagar
m. Jalpaiguri, trade center of West Bengal state
n. Koch Behar, former capital of petty kingdom that was a gateway to Assam
o. Gauhati (Assam), most developed city of Assam and one site of ancient Kamarupa civilization
p. Tezpur, important trade and transport town
q. North Lakhimpur, gateway town to the Dafla Hills of Arunachal Pradesh
r. Dibrugarh, market center on the Brahmaputra
s. Sadiya, crossroads of trade routes connecting to Tibet, Burma and Assam
t. Teju, gateway town to the upper Burmese hills
3. The Indian bazaar style of North plains:
   a. one main street with a few inter-connecting lanes
   b. clustered houses
   c. ground floors filled with shops, with families living upstairs
   d. new government offices in cement buildings
   e. streets crowded with buses, trucks, bullock carts, pedestrians
   f. Marwari merchants now dominate major sectors of modern markets

D. Pilgrimage centers
   1. Hindu/Buddhist traditions reach into the region
      a. sites across northern reaches of the Ganges are important to Buddhism
      b. region figures prominantly in Hindu mythology and in the epics (*Ramayana, puranas*)
      c. development of tantric traditions on the Gangetic frontier, especially Assam
   2. Important sites
      a. Haridwar, site of the extremely popular yearly Hindu festival, the *Khumbamela*
      b. Rishikesh, a town where almost every major Hindu sect has an ashram

c. Devaprayag, confluence of the Bhagirathi (upper Ganges) and Mandakini
d. Lumbini, birthplace of the Buddha in modern Nepal, rediscovered in the late nineteenth century, now dotted with Buddhist monasteries from countries all over the world
e. Janakpur, site associated with the *Ramayana*
f. Varaha Kshetra, confluence site on the Sapta Kosi river associated with Vishnu in his boar incarnation
g. Hajo/Kamakhya, ancient pilgrimage site near Gauhati, sacred to Devi; a major *shakti pitha* in the Hindu tradition, and now center of many religious shrines
h. Sibsagar, site of important Shiva temple in Assam

IV. Social Relations

A. In Nepal and Assam, constant in-migration, accelerating in recent years, has given rise to extremely mixed villages and the greatest ethnic diversity in the Himalayan region

B. With the coming of the Shah state in Nepal, lowland tribals in increasing interaction with Pahari peoples from the hills and Indians from the south

C. Ethnic Group Populations (See Map 7)
   1. Tharu
   2. Bura
   3. Bodo speakers
      a. Dhimal
      b. Koche
      c. Rajbansis/Meche
      d. Kachari
   4. Danuwar & Majhi
   5. Satar/Santal
   6. Fishing peoples
      a. living on larger river ecological niches
      b. in Nepal, called "Bhote"
   7. Recent migrants
      a. Indo-Aryan: Paharis, Biharis, Bengalis
      b. Tibeto-Burmans: Newars, Limbu, Rai, Tamang, Gurung, etc.
   8. Muslims
      a. western regions: 20 % of population
      b. Nepal: less than 1 %
      c. Assam/West Bengal: 25% of population

Narayani River, Chitwan, Nepal

Terai House, Nepal

Kachari House, Assam

126

D. Social Organization
1. Castes and ethnic groups typically divided into named sub-divisions associated with specific localities
2. Non-caste society
   a. tribal kinship patterns emphasizing clan affiliation predominate
   b. close kin cooperation and reciprocity
   c. clan leadership based on seniority
   d. patrilineal kinship system, virilocal residence
3. Caste society
   a. standard hierarchy:
      Bahun (Brahman)
      Rajput
      Chetri
      Cultivating castes
      Occupational castes
   b. Relations based on high caste dominance and economic interdependence
   c. *jajmani* system relating specialists (priests, artisans, service castes) to patrons
   d. purity and pollution norms regulate interaction
   e. patrilineal kinship system, virilocal residence
4. At the village level, usual high caste dominance, especially in terms of land ownership and tenantry/sharecropping
5. Pattern of tribal peoples adopting caste names and entering the caste Hindu realm of social discourse

E. Political Relations
1. Dominant groups
   a. Himachal Pradesh and Uttar Pradesh: *Rajput/Brahman*
   b. Nepal: *Bahun/Thakuri/Chetri*
   c. Sikkim and Bhutan: monastic control of lowland populations
   d. Assam: Ahom descendants
   e. Marwari economic importance throughout the region
2. Processes of social dominance
   a. Sanskritization: Hindu/tribal continuum, with tribals integrated at the bottom end of the caste hierarchy
   b. little Buddhist influence among lowland populations
   c. history of hill rulers, bureaucrats, and businessmen exploiting less sophisticated Terai peoples
3. Formal political articulation
   a. educated elites form as central government bureaucracy grows
   b. on village level, peasantry organized by *panchayat* councils

4. Conflict and resistance
   a. language and cultural movements in Assam, e.g. the "Bodo Autonomous Republic" formed to resist assimilation with the Assamese
   b. tribal groups attempting to raise their caste status (e.g. from "Koche" to "Rajbansis")
   c. Nepali migrants in submontane organizing to demand a separate "Gorkhaland" in West Bengal
   d. *sukumbasi* movement: groups of landless people settling on unoccupied lands
   e. squatters in major towns

V. Cultural Continuities

A. Languages

1. Indo-Aryan family
   a. Hindi-Urdu
   b. Punjabi
   c. Dogri
   d. Awadhi
   e. Bhojpuri
   f. Maithili
   g. Bihari
   h. Bengali
   i. Nepali
   j. Assamese
2. Tibeto-Burman
   a. Kachari
   b. Boro
   c. Mechi
   d. Dhimali
3. Dravidian languages
4. Mid-hill Tibeto-Burman languages of migrants
5. The widespread Tharu dialects have not yet been classified with any of the above groups; all now reflect heavy Indic influences

B. Religious Traditions

1. Hinduism
   a. worship of Vishnu, Shiva, Devi, Krishna
   b. performance of life cycle rites requiring a Brahman priest
   c. major festivals: *Dashara* (also called: *Dasain, Durga Puja*), *Diwali* (*Tihar*), *Tij*, and *Holi*
   d. formation of traditions at important pilgrimage sites of the western and central regions

1. e.g. *Khumbamelas* held at Haridwar each year and
   especially the twelve year *mela* that draws millions of
   holy men and pilgrims for sacred bathing at the
   auspicious moment
2. e.g. yearly festival at Kamakhya
   e. *Bairagi mandals*: networks of *sadhu* communities of the lineage
      originating with Svami Ramananda, a 14th Century Vaishnava
      guru
   f. In Assam, the Vaisnava mass movement initiated by
      Shankaradeva (1486-1568)
      1. supported and simplified caste relations
      2. introduced monastic religious institutions called *sattras*
         that organize the religious hierarchy and maintain
         communal devotion
   g. *bharavas* among the western Tharus: *mantra* masters who apply
      Sanskritic tradition to the local pantheon, invoke Kali to subdue
      demons
   h. Gorakhnath worship among the Rajbanshis and others
   i. importance of Hindu astrologers in everyday life
2. Spirit cults maintained by mediums: *ojhas, jhankris*, etc.
3. Ancestor cults to lineage deities, often centered in household shrine
   a. Koch/Kachari worship the deity Bethan in the form of a
      poinsettia tree (*siju*)
   b. Tharu officiant, the *ghar guruva*, conducts annual sacrifices to
      lineage deities
4. Locality deities specific to village boundaries, jungle, rivers,
   mountaintops, animals
5. Karma belief among Indianized peoples
6. Cult of *mithan* sacrifice in the eastern region
   a. animals sacrificed for household prosperity, especially children,
      good harvests, plentiful herds
   b. special sites constructed where forked sacrificial posts and
      crania are displayed
   c. cultural continuity with peoples of SE Asia
7. Worship of Muslim saints called *pirs*

C. Cultural Processes and Continuities
   1. Sanskritization -- the preeminence of Hindu tradition in Nepal and
      Assam remains a chief cultural characteristic though modern changes
      continually alter the exact nature of Brahmanical influence
   2. "Nationalization"
      a. Nepalization of Tarai
      b. Bhutanese isolationism
      c. Assamese separatism
   3. Christian missions in the northeast

4. Area known for syncretistic practices blending Muslim, Hindu, Sikh, and local traditions
5. Peoples often accent their ethnic group and local boundaries by emphasizing indigenous traits and adopting distinctive combinations from the possibilities above
6. Distinctive aspects of the material culture
   a. dress styles, jewelry, and special foods prominent ethnic group markers
   b. strong North Indian influences
   c. adaptations to the summer heat in clothing, architecture

Mustard Fields, Nepalese Terai

Recommended Readings and References

Bista, Dor Bahadur. "The Tharu," in *People of Nepal*. Kathmandu: Ratna Pustak Bandhar, 1972.

Burling, Robbins. *Rengsanggri: Family and Kinship in a Garo Village*. Philadelphia: University of Pennsylvania Press, 1963.

Cantlie, Audrey. *The Assamese*. London: Curzon Press, 1984.

_____. "Vaishnava Reform Sects in Assam," in Richard Barghart and Andrey Cantlie eds. *Indian Religion*. New York: St. Martins, 1985, 134-157.

Chauhan, S.K. "Caste Structure in Assam," *Eastern Anthropologist* 26 (2), 1976, 173-182.

Clark, R.C. *Rajbangshis of North Bengal*. Hartford Seminary: Unpublished Ph.D. Dissertation, 1979.

Eliot, Sir Charles N.E. "Hinduism in Assam," *Journal of the Royal Asiatic Society*, 1910, 1164-1180.

Gaige, Frederick. *Regionalism and Nationalism in Nepal*. Berkeley: University of California Press, 1972.

Ghimire, Premlata. "The Individual and Group Identities of the Sapha Hod," in Maheshwar P. Joshi, Allen C. Fanger, and Charles W. Brown eds. *Himalaya: Past and Present*. Almora: Shree Almora Book Depot, 1990.

McDougal, Charles. *Village and Household Economy in Far Western Nepal*. Kirtipur: Tribhuvan University, 1968.

Rose, Leo E. and Margaret W. Fisher. *The Northeast Frontier Agency of India*. U. S. Government Department of State: Publication 8288, 1967.

Siiger, Halfdan. "The Boro of Assam," *Ethnological Field-Research in Chitral, Sikkim, and Assam*. Copenhagen, 1956.

Simoons, F.J. *The Ceremonial Ox of India*. Madison: University of Wisconsin Press, 1968.

Srivastava, S.K. *The Tharus*: *A Study in Culture Dynamics*. Agra University Press, 1958.

Stonor, Charles. "Notes on the Religion and Ritual among the Dafla Tribes of the Assam Himalayas," *Anthropos* 52, 1957, 1-23.

Rural Settlements, Central Nepal

Chapter 11

MID-MONTANE PAHARI REGION

I. Physical Geography

A. Map location: middle hills from 2,500 - 7,500 ft beginning east of Kashmir through the Panjab hills, Garhwal, Kumaon, Jumla, and central Nepal; considerable overlap from west of the Kathmandu Valley to the eastern Nepalese hills; extends up routes leading to great Hindu pilgrimage sites in the highland regions

B. Topography
1. Mahabharata Lekh and subsidiary ridges from the high Himalayas
2. Terrain dominated by high ridges and steep river valleys
3. Watersheds:
   a. tributaries of the Indus
   b. tributaries of the Ganges

C. Climate
1. Temperate monsoon climate, with wide micro-climactic variations
2. Most areas inhabitable all year
3. Monsoon rainfall decreases as one moves west from Assam

D. Flora & fauna
1. Until recent years, settlements separated by extensive temperate forestlands, especially with sal, other hardwoods, and conifers
2. Rhododendron and bamboo stands common
3. Wildlife includes leopards, several deer species, bears, monkeys, boar, blue sheep

E. Communications networks
1. River valleys provide the best passage in many places
2. Trade routes connected to the trans-Himalayan passes

II. Subsistance and Trade Patterns

A. Ecological micro-environments have led to a wide spectrum of subsistence strategies that vary according to altitude, daily sunlight, local winds, water availability, and household resources

B. Hunter-gatherers, once common in the region, survive now in only the most remote places
   1. Raute
   2. Kusunda

C. Agricultural production
   1. Most households depend primarily on subsistence agriculture and live within a fragile balance of grain production, animal husbandry, and some means of obtaining cash income
   2. Kitchen vegetable gardens for household consumption
   3. Shifting agriculturalists (*jhum*)
      a. slash and burn agriculture on a multi-year cyclic system
      b. few remain due to state prohibitions
   4. Settled agriculturalists
      a. monsoon season grain crops:
         1. paddy rice, grown in the few areas where irrigated river bottomland is sufficient
         2. dry rice, corn, grown in land terraced to catch wet season rains
      b. winter season crops
         1. sometimes alternated on monsoon lands
         2. hearty varieties:
            a. wheat
            b. barley
            c. millet
            d. buckwheat
      c. cash crops
         1. mustard (oil seeds)
         2. hashish
         3. tobacco
         4. citrus
      d. prosperous families purchase spices, lentils, and other foods to make the diet more nutritious and varied

D. Animal Husbandry
   1. Cow and/or water buffalo
      a. essential to the subsistence farmer's adaptation
      b. they graze on stubble between growing seasons, but must eat fodder collected by household at other times
   2. Goats and sheep
      a. small herds are important in some areas
      b. most herds are brought down from the highlands in the cold season; exchanges with lower altitude peoples -- grazing rights for animal products or cash -- mark such relationships

134

   c. common herders:
    1. Gaddis of Himachal Pradesh
    2. Gujjars of Jammu and Kashmir, Himachal Pradesh,
     Uttar Pradesh

F. Trade

1. Local trade: patterns of exchange between upland herders and mid-montane agriculturalists: wool, salt, animal products ↔grain, consumer goods
2. Ritual friendships (*mit*) follow inter-ethnic group trade relations
3. Retail trade in products from outside the region

G. Wage labor & Migration

1. In many places, the remittances from men working outside the region are essential to maintaining local subsistence economy
  a. jobs in urban India
  b. army employment for India and Britain
2. Labor exchanges between households during peak agricultural seasons support those who must plant, weed, and harvest the monsoon crops
3. Short-term portering for tourists and pilgrims provides cash income for younger men

III. Settlement Patterns

A. Historical Background

1. For the last three thousand years, plains peoples have moved into the hills
2. In certain areas, Tibetanized peoples and Tibetan Buddhist institutions extended far into the mid- montane region
3. Era of Muslim conquest of the Gangetic plain (1000-1600 AD) was likely a period of heavy plains-hills migration
4. West to east migration by Indianized hill peoples has led to the displacement and/or absorption of Tibeto-Burman peoples
5. The Gorkhali conquest
  a. introduced Nepali domination from Chamba to Sikkim for a short period (1775-1817)
  b. encouraged entrepreneurs to spread from the center of the new state into the conquered zones to mine, mint, collect taxes, etc.
  c. caused conquered peoples to flee eastward to avoid taxation and/or enslavement

B. Village Settlements

1. General tendency to be found in well-watered areas, near lands suited for agriculture, and, often, fortification
2. Indian and Nepalese villages: usually hamletted by caste/ethnic identity in dispersed settlements

3. Sometimes Paharis live in close proximity to Tibeto-Burman hamlets
4. House styles vary regionally
    a. In higher areas, stone walls, slate roof, two-storey houses
    b. At lower altitudes, mud walls and thatch (or tile) roofs
    c. wealthier families build larger dwellings, ornament them with carved wooden windows and doors, and use baked tile or corrugated metal roofing

C. Political and commercial centers
    1. Major towns
        a. Chamba, former capital of an ancient kingdom once closely linked to Kashmir
        b. Dharamsala, current center for the Dalai Lama's government in exile, a center of refugee Tibetan culture
        c. Nagar, old capital of the Kulu kingdom
        d. Mandi, seat of a former kingdom
        e. Simla, the hill station built for the British to be the summer capital of the Raj
        f. Mussoorie, British hill station constructed in 1827
        g. Nainital, resort town built around a glacial lake
        h. Almora, former capital of a small Hindu kingdom
        i. Jumla, the most important district center in western Nepal
        j. Baglung, once a mining center, still a major entrepot on the Gandaki trade route
        k. Pokhara, an old Newar town situated alongside a glacial lake that is now a center of trade and tourism
        l. Gorkha, home of the Shah family that currently rules Nepal
    2. In Nepal, *hat bazaars*, periodic markets, held at designated sites, often near government centers
    3. Some towns develop as army garrisons to guard the passes, especially from the Indian plains into the hills

D. Pilgrimage centers --
    1. Major sites:
        a. Amarnath, a cave the state of Jammu and Kashmir that encloses a Shiva "*Hima linga*" formed by ice
        b. Jwalamukti, natural gas flame location in northwest Himachal Pradesh, sacred to Devi
        c. Triloknath, Shiva site in northwest Himachal Pradesh
        d. Yamunotri, headwaters of the Yamuna, sacred to Vishnu
        e. Uttarkashi, site centered around Shiva Vishvanath temple
        f. Gangotri, headwaters of the Ganges, sacred to Shiva; the main temple was built by a Gurkha general in the late eighteenth century

g. Hemkhand Lake, a Sikh site sacred to the memory of the Tenth Guru, Govind Singh

h. Kedarnath, site sacred to Shiva in Uttar Pradesh

i. Badrinath, the most important Vishnava shrine in the Himalayan region

j. Vishnu Prayag, confluence of the Alakanda and Leti rivers in Garhwal

k. Nanda Prayag, confluence of the Alakanda and Nanda rivers

l. Karna Prayag, confluence of the Alakanda and Pindar rivers in Almora district

m. Rudra Prayag, confluence of the Mandakini and Alakanda Rivers in Tehri district

n. Garhi, site of Tapkeshwar Mahadeva temple

o. Muktinath, site on the upper Gandaki with burning natural gas fissures and 108 waterspouts; predominantly Saivite, but sacred to Hindus and Buddhists

p. Salagrama (also called Damodarkund), source of *salagrams*, black fossilized stones sacred to Vishnu that are worshipped throughout India

q. Ridi, a town between Palpa and Baglung, "A Benares for Paharis"

r. Pashupatinath, complex in the Kathmandu Valley devoted to Shiva as "Lord of Creatures"

2. In every area, there are pilgrimage sites of regional importance, especially sacred mountains and river confluences

IV. Social Relations

A. Ethnic Group Populations (See Map 8)

1. The Pahari or Parbatiya, the numerically dominant Hindu peoples who are organized in castes (*jat*)

a. General hierarchy:
> *Brahman (Bahun)*
> *Rajput/Thakuri*
> *Chetri*
> *Gaddi*
> *Khas-Pahari*
> *Gharti*, former slaves
> *Dom*: Occupational castes
> > *Damai*- tailors
> > *Kami*- smith
> > *Sarki*- shoemaker

b. any regional ranking will vary and local individuals disagree on the specific orderings

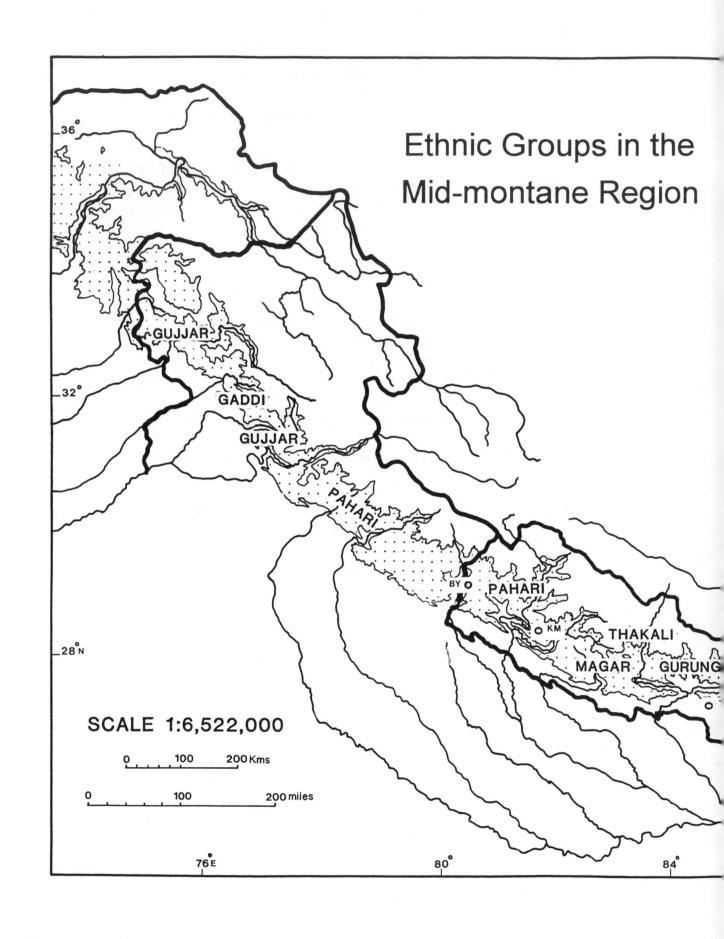

Ethnic Groups in the
Mid-montane Region

GUJJAR

GADDI

GUJJAR

PAHARI

BY ○ PAHARI

○ KM

THAKALI

MAGAR GURUNG

SCALE 1:6,522,000

0 ____ 100 ____ 200 Kms

0 ____ 100 ____ 200 miles

36°

32°

28°N

76°E   80°   84°

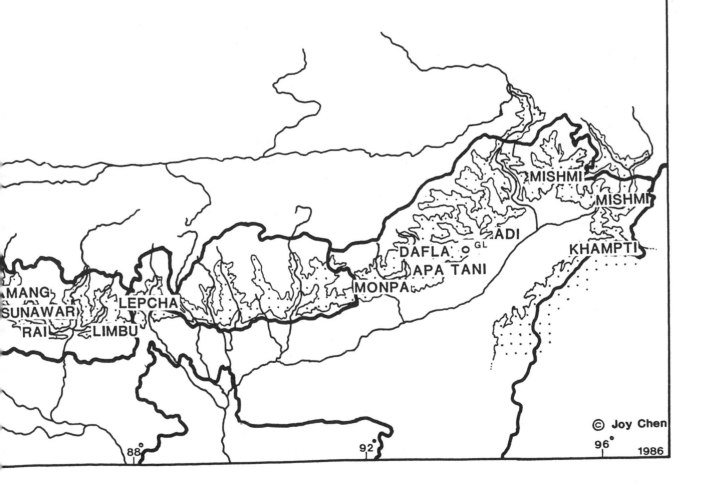

8

BY— BYANGSHI
GL— GALONG
KM— KHAM MAGAR
NE— NEWAR
PA— PAHARI
TA— TAMANG

feet   meters

8202   2500

2297   700

MISHMI

MISHMI

ADI

DAFLA ○ GL

KHAMPTI

APA TANI

MONPA

MANG

SUNAWAR   LEPCHA

RAI   LIMBU

© Joy Chen

88°   92°   96°

1986

      c. in Nepal, *Bahun-Chetris* have the highest fertility rate among all ethnic groups

   2. Tibeto-Burman peoples who live in areas of overlap
      a. central hills: Kham Magar, Magar, Gurung, Thakali, Tamang, Newar, "Pahari Newar"
      b. eastern hills: Limbu, Rai
   3. In many areas, ethnic groups have separate yet overlapping ways of life

B. Social Organization

   1. Castes and ethnic groups typically divided into named sub-divisions associated with specific localities
   2. Caste society
      a. follows general four *varna* order
      b. purity and pollution norms regulate interaction between castes
      c. *jajmani* system regulates artisan - patron relations
      d. In Nepalese areas, a three-fold caste division of the Shah legal codes won recognition:
         1. *tagadhari*, "thread wearers"
         2. *matwali*, "liquor drinking peoples"
         3. *achut*, "untouchables"
      e. Pahari caste practices are less orthodox and orthoprax when compared to plains practices (See Chapter 16)
      f. patrilineal kinship system, with virilocal residence
      g. access to hearth area and commensual relations key indicators of relative status
   3. Tibeto-Burman groups ranked at lower levels in caste society
      a. most are *matwali*
      b. observance of Brahmanical norms
         1. some ethnic groups have adopted caste practices
         2. this may vary within the same group across a given region
      c. See Tibeto-Burman chapter

C. Political Relations

   1. Dominant groups
      a. India: *Brahman/Thakuri/Rajput*
      b. Nepal: *Bahun/Chetri, Thakuri*
   2. Processes of social dominance
      a. Sanskritization -- emulation of high caste norms
         1. India: high caste, literate Hindus with access to political power
         2. Nepal: Gorkhali conquest and *Muluki Ain* law codes favored high castes and those with royal connections
         3. Observing norms of Hindu orthodoxy often facilitates political ambitions in the hills
         4. Restricting prestigious Hindu observances maintains high caste claims to superior status and power

Multi-ethnic Village, Central Nepal

      b. State land grants in Nepal gave allies of the ruling elite the basis for acquiring further wealth

      c. access to elite education

3. Political articulation

      a. client-patron relations dominate village, district, and national affairs

      b. connections with new government institutions give access to special privilege

      c. institutions of local, state, and national government organize polities in new configurations

      d. voting a new factor in local power relations

      e. in the face of plains incursions into local life, being a "Pahari", i.e. "hill man", has provided an element of regional identification and solidarity

  4. Conflict and resistance
    a. caste and ethnic group organizations involved in various issues:
      1. survival of local traditions, especially language
      2. group uplift and access to special opportunities
      3. lowest castes rejecting traditional roles and prejudicial treatment by high castes
    b. ecological movements to preserve the integrity of local environments
      1. Chipko, a movement to save Himalayan forests
      2. resistance to large hydro-electric projects

V. Cultural Continuities

 A. Major Indic Languages
  1. Hindi-Urdu
  2. Gaddi
  3. Pahari
    a. west (Garwali)
    b. central (Kumaoni)
    c. east (Nepali)

 B. Religious Traditions
  1. Hinduism
    a. overall, the religious traditions are quite similiar to those described among Hindus of northern India
    b. temples with land endowments are major institutions
    c. Pahari Brahmans
      1. families linked by priestly initiation, training, and religious alliances
      2. common division by nature of service:
        a. pandit
        b. life-cycle ritualist
        c. death rite ritualist
    d. worship of Vishnu, Shiva, Devi
    e. performance of life-cycle rites, *samskaras*
    f. celebration of major festivals
      1. *Dashara (Dasain)*
      2. *Diwali (Tihar)*
      3. *Holi*
      4. *Tij*
      5. *Mahasivaratri*

g. formation of traditions at important pilgrimage localities at auspicious times each year
    1. e.g. Amarnath pilgrimage in summer draws thousands from across India each year who trek up to the ice cave in Kashmir
    2. e.g. visits to Pashupati (Nepal) to attend the *Shivaratri* festival, "the night of Shiva", in winter
h. common mythology of high Indic deities dominating local spirit cults
i. importance of astrology
j. represented by Hindu monasteries such as the *kutis*, institutions of NW Nepal associated with the Giri branch of the Shankaracarya order

2. Buddhism
  a. few remnants of Buddhist institutions
  b. partial survivals seen in old temples and in certain oracular cults (Jumla)
  c. since 1959, Tibetan refugee institutions have been built across the region, with the government in exile in Dharamsala

3. Spirit cults involved in exorcism and healing
  a. Shamans
    1. *jhankris*
    2. *dom* of Uttar Pradesh
    3. *dhamis* associated with small spirit buildings, *khotans* (Nepal)
  b. oracles
  c. Brahman exorcists in Kumaon and western Nepal

4. Ancestor cults to lineage deities (*kul devatas*) maintained by families

5. Karma belief among Indicized peoples

C. Cultural Processes and Continuities

1. Sanskritization
  a. the preeminence of Hindu tradition in India and Nepal has led to the spread of the cultural complex dominated by the Brahmanical pantheon, ritualism, and social norms
  b. Nepalese government sponsoring Sanskrit schools

2. Nationalization
  a. integration of Indian Himalayan regions into the plains economic and political system
  b. Nepal also dominated by India economically, but in the political evolution of Nepal's rural areas, the polity focuses internally toward Kathmandu

3. Westernization
  a. elites imitate Western fashions, tastes, education
  b. alliances with international development agencies

4. Peoples often accent their ethnic group and locality boundaries by emphasizing distinctive indigenous traits and adopting unique combinations from the possibilities cited above
5. Distinctive aspects of material culture
   a. dress styles, jewelry, and specialty foods are prominent ethnic group markers
   b. sweetened tea with milk
   c. rice beer, chang, and distilled rice spirits, *raksi*
   d. Pahari men wear *daura-suruval* ("pants-coat") and *topi* hat on formal occasions and carry the curved knife, the *khukuri*

Pahari Homestead amidst Corn Fields, Central Nepal

Recommended Readings and References

Bennett, Lynn. *Dangerous Wives and Sacred Sisters: Social and Symbolic Roles of High-Caste Women in Nepal.* NY: Columbia University Press, 1983.

Berreman, Gerald D. *Hindus of the Himalayas.* Berkeley: University of California Press, 1972.

Brown, Charles W. and Joshi, Maheshwar P. "Caste Dynamics and Fluidity in the Historical Anthropology of Kumaon," in Maheshwar P. Joshi, Allen C. Fanger, and Charles W. Brown eds. *Himalaya: Past and Present.* Almora: Shree Almora Book Depot, 1990.

Campbell, J. Gabriel. *Saints and Householders.* Kathmandu: Ratna Pustak Bhandar, 1976.

Caplan, Lionel. *Administration and Politics in a Nepalese Town.* Oxford University Press, 1975.

Caplan, Patricia. "Ascetics in Western Nepal," *Eastern Anthropologist* 26 (2), 1976, 173-182.

Fanger, Allen C. *Diachronic and Synchronic Perspectives on Kumaoni Society and Culture.* Ann Arbor: University Microfilms International, 1980.

Gray, John N. "Hypergamy, Kinship and Caste among the Chettris of Nepal," *Contributions to Indian Sociology* 14 (1), 1980, 1-33.

Gurung, Harka. *Nepal: Main Ethnic and Caste Groups by District.* Kathmandu, 1994.

Hitchcock, John T. "Himalayan Ecology and Family Religious Variation," in George Kurian ed. *The Family in India: A Regional View.* The Hague: Mouton, 1974.

Narayan, Kirin. "Birds on a Branch: Girlfriends and Wedding Songs in Kangra," *Ethos* 14 (1), 1986, 47-75.

Newell, William H. "An Upper Ravi Village: The Process of Social Change in Himachal Pradesh," in K. Ishwaran ed. *Change and Continuity in India's Villages.* New York: Columbia University Press, 1970.

Parry, Jonathan P. *Caste and Kinship in Kangra.* Boston: Routledge and Kegan Paul, 1979.

Prindle, Peter Hodge. *Tinglatar: Socio-economic Relationships of a Brahmin Village of East Nepal.* Kathmandu: Ratna Pustak Bhandar, 1983.

_____. "The Jajmani System: a Nepalese Example," *Journal of Anthropological Research* 53 (3), 1977, 290-301.

Rosser, Colin. "A `Hermit' Village in Kulu," in M.N. Srinivas ed. *India's Villages.* New Delhi: Asia Publishing, 1968.

Sanwal, Rami. *Social Statification in Rural Kumaon.* Delhi: Oxford University Press, 1976.

Sax, William S. *Mountain Goddess: Gender and Politics in a Himalayan Pilgrimage.* New York: Oxford University Press, 1991.

Stone, Linda. *Illness and Healing in Central Nepal.* Lewiston: Edwin Mellon Press, 1987.

Gurung Settlement, Central Nepal

Chapter 12

MID-MONTANE TIBETO-BURMAN REGION

I. Physical Geography

A. Map location: hills from 2,500 - 7,500 feet from west Nepal across to West Bengal, Sikkim, and Bhutan to Arunachal Pradesh

B. Topography
1. Mahabharata Lekh and subsidiary ridges from the high Himalayas
2. Terrain dominated by high ridges and steep river valleys
3. Watersheds:
     a. eastern tributaries of the Ganges
     b. tributaries of the Brahmaputra

C. Climate
1. Temperate climate, with wide micro-climactic variations
2. Most areas inhabitable all year
3. Monsoon rainfall heaviest in the Assam region, and generally decreases as one moves west

D. Flora and fauna
1. Until recent years, settlements separated by large forest tracts, especially of sal and other hardwoods; large stands still exist in Bhutan and Arunachal Pradesh
2. Bamboo common in many places and put to many uses
3. Wildlife includes several deer species, bears, snow leopards, blue sheep, monkeys, wild boar

E. Communications networks
1. River valleys provide the best means of north-south passage in many places
2. Routes connecting with major trans-Himalayan routes are of special significance

II. Subsistance and Trade Patterns

A. Ecological micro-environments create a wide spectrum of subsistence formuli that vary according to altitude, daily sunlight, local winds, water availability, and household resources

B. Hunters and gatherers, once common in the region, may survive now in only the most remote places

C. Agricultural production
    1. Most households depend primarily on subsistence agriculture and live within a fragile balance of grain production, animal husbandry, and some means of obtaining cash income
    2. Kitchen vegetable gardens for household consumption
    3. Shifting agriculturalists
        a. slash and burn agriculture (*jhum*), on a multi-year cyclic system, exists where populations are most sparse
        b. few remain due to state prohibitions
        c. until 1965, Tamangs and Gurungs of the Pokhara region still practiced *jhum* and burned the forests in communal groups
    4. Settled agriculturalists
        a. monsoon season grain crops:
            1. paddy rice, grown in the few areas where irrigated river bottomland is sufficient
            2. dry rice, corn, grown in land terraced to catch wet season rains
        b. winter season crops
            1. sometimes alternated on monsoon lands
            2. hearty varieties:
                a. wheat
                b. barley
                c. millet
                d. buckwheat
        c. cash crops
            1. mustard (oil seeds)
            2. hashish
            3. tobacco
            4. tea
            5. cardamon
            6. citrus
        d. prosperous families purchase spices, lentils, and other foods to make the diet more nutritious and varied

D. Animal Husbandry
    1. Cow and/or water buffalo
        a. essential to the subsistence farmer's adaptation
        b. graze on stubble between growing seasons, but must eat fodder collected by household at other times
    2. Goats and sheep
        a. small herds are important in some areas

        b. most herds are brought from the highlands in the cold season; exchange -- grazing rights for animal products and/or cash -- marks such relationships

        c. some households contract with herdsmen to take animals to and from summer pastures

    3. Some ethnic groups of Arunachal Pradesh are not milk users, e.g. the Dafla, Miri, Apa Tani, Adi

E. Trade

1. Local trade: patterns of exchange between upland herders and mid-montane agriculturalists wool, salt animal products ↔ grain, consumer goods
2. Ritual friendships (*mit*) follow inter-ethnic group trade relations
3. Retail trade in products from outside the region

F. Wage labor & Migration

1. In many places, the remittance income from men working outside the region is essential to maintaining local subsistence
    a. jobs in urban India
    b. army employment for India and Britain
2. Labor exchanges between households during peak agricultural seasons support those who must plant, weed, and harvest the monsoon crops
3. Short-term portering for tourists and pilgrims provides cash income for younger men
4. Pensions an important source of cash in many areas

III. Settlement Patterns

A. Historical background

1. For centuries, plains peoples and peoples from the highlands as far as NW and SW China have moved into the hills
2. In certain areas, Tibetan peoples and Buddhist monasteries extended far over into the mid-montane region
3. More recent migration by Indianized hill peoples has moved from west to east and has likely led to the displacement of Tibeto-Burman peoples
4. There has also been the conversion of Tibeto-Burman ethnic groups to a Pahari identity
    a. through inter-marriage
    b. by adopting Brahmanical socio-cultural norms and caste-designated names
5. The Gorkhali conquest
    a. introduced Nepali rule from Chamba to Sikkim for a short period (1775-1817)

  b. encouraged entrepreneurs to migrate from the center of the new state into the conquered zones to mine, mint, collect taxes, acquire land, etc.

  c. caused some conquered peoples to flee eastward to avoid slavery and/or heavy taxation

  d. modern laws ended communal land holdings (*kipat*) in 1968

 6. Indo-Chinese war of 1962 in northeast leads to a vast increase in Indian nation's involvement across Arunachal Pradesh and Assam

B. Village Settlements

1. General tendency to find villages in well-watered areas, near lands suitable for agriculture and, often, fortification
2. Indian hills and Nepal: continuous succession of dispersed multi-caste settlements, hamletted according to ethnic/caste boundaries
3. Sometimes Paharis live in close proximity to Tibeto-Burman hamlets
4. House styles vary regionally:
 a. In upland areas, stone walls, slate roof, two- storey houses
 b. In lower altitudes, mud walls and thatch (or tile) roof, two-storey houses
 c. some houses in eastern region raised on wooden piles
 d. wealthier families build larger dwellings, ornament them with carved wooden windows and doors, and use baked tile or corrugated metal roofing

C. Political and commercial centers

1. Major towns
 a. For the Kathmandu Valley towns, see Chapter 12
 b. Okhaldunga, an administrative town on north- south trade route
 c. Dhankuta, a large bazaar and administrative town in eastern Nepal
 d. Bhojpur, important market town
 e. Chainpur, town known for Newar metalworkers
 f. Taplejung, administrative and market center
 g. Ilam, center of Nepal's tea industry
 h. Darjeeling, hill station and important tea center of West Bengal
 i. Kalimpong, gateway city to Bhutan and Sikkim
 j. Gangtok, former capital of Sikkim
 k. Ziro, capital of Arunachal Pradesh state, home region of the Apa Tani
 l. Bomdila, market town of western Arunachal
 m. Hapoli, market town of the Dafla hills
 n. Nyeying, chief city of the Abor Hills
2. In Nepal, *hat bazar*, periodic markets, are held at designated sites, often near government centers

D. Pilgrimage centers
   1. In every area, there are important regional pilgrimage sites, especially sacred mountains and river confluences
   2. A few are sites of yearly shaman festivals
   3. Important Buddhist monasteries in Sikkim and Bhutan
   4. No major all-India pilgrimage centers in the eastern hills, a contrast with the western hills

IV. Social Relations

A. Ethnic Group Populations (See Map 8)
   1. Major Tibeto-Burman Ethnic Groups (west to east:)
      a. Byangshi
      b. Kham Magar
      c. Magar
      d. Gurung
      e. Thakali
      f. Newar
      g. Sunuwar
      h. "Kiranti"
         1. Rai
         2. Limbu
      i. Thami
      j. Lepcha
      k. Monpa
      l. Apa Tani
      m. Dafla
      n. Miri
      o. Adi
      p. Galong
      q. Mishmi
      r. Khampti
   2. The Pahari (or Parbatiya) Hindu peoples found in certain areas
      a. Standard hierarchy:
         Brahmin (Bahun)
         Thakuri
         Chetri
         Gharti, former slaves
         Dom, occupational castes
            Damai-tailors
            Kami-smith
            Sarki-shoemaker
      b. Regional ranking will vary from this model and local individuals will disagree regarding the exact order

B. Social Organization
   1. Castes and ethnic groups typically divided into named sub-divisions associated with specific localities
   2. Tibeto-Burman societies
      a. kinship patterns centered in exogamous clans
      b. compared to Pahari peoples, social relations within ethnic groups tend to be reciprocal, egalitarian and communal
      c. male clan elders uphold customary order
         1. manage communal land ownership and forest resources
         2. mediate disputes in the local community
         3. approve marriage liasons
      d. women have fewer restrictions than Pahari women
      e. Tibeto-Burman groups ranked at lower levels of caste society
      f. common two-division hierarchy in some ethnic groups between "nobles" and "commoners"
         1. Gurung "*car jat*" vs. "*sora jat*"
         2. Tamang "four clans" vs. "sixteen clans"
         3. Newar castes "*la cale ju pim*" vs "*la cale maju pim*"
         4. Apa Tani
      g. institutions that are distinctive to certain ethnic groups
         1. *rodighar*, a fellowship of same-generation young men and women that meets in a special house for socializing and working; common in Gurung areas, but once found among the Thakalis and Tamangs
         2. *dhikur*: rotating credit associations that help petty traders to raise capital (See Chapter 2)
         3. *guthi*: institutions organized around a particular temple, religious ritual, cult that may have similiar functions as dhikur
         4. Work exchange groups, with one representative from each household, oriented toward the labor intensive tasks of the agricultural season
   3. Caste societies
      a. purity and pollution norms regulate interaction between castes
      b. high caste domination of social sphere
      c. see Pahari Chapter
   4. In many areas, Tibeto-Burman groups and Pahari groups have "separate yet overlapping" ways of life

C. Political Relations
   1. Dominant groups
      a. pan-regional pattern: Tibeto-Burman ethnic group leaders act as middlemen with state administration (e.g. Rai *subbas*)

b. Nepal: *Bahun/Chetri, Thakuri*; Newar merchants; *subbas* (regional administrators); *mukhiyas* (village representatives to land revenue authorities)

c. Sikkim: Bhutia/Buddhist clergy and later Nepali settlers

d. Bhutan: Buddhist clergy and royal family

e. Arunachal Pradesh: ethnic group leaders act as middlemen with state administration

2. Processes of social dominance

    a. Sanskritization --

        1. India: high caste, literate Hindus with access to political power

        2. Nepal: Gorkhali conquest and *Muluki Ain* law codes favored high castes and those with wealth

        3. conformity to Hindu orthodoxy often facilitates political ambition

        4. high motivation for Tibeto-Burman groups to adapt on every level of social and cultural importance

        5. the pressure to find a place in the system of caste ranking resulted in considerable ethnic amalgamation and the consolidation of certain Tibeto-Burman groups

    b. Nationalization

        1. land grants in Nepal gave allies of the Gorkha state basis for acquiring further wealth

        2. ending communal land holdings changes Tibeto-Burman societies formerly tied to clan-based systems of land allotment and control

        3. in Sikkim, Assam, and Arunachal Pradesh, integration with India, especially with Tibeto-Burman groups designated as "Scheduled Castes"

        4. Adaptation to Bhutanese rule

    c. Tibetanization in some areas:

        1. dominance by monasteries and highland Buddhist traditions

        2. monastic landlords allied with local clan chiefs

        3. Political articulation

            a. connections with new government institutions, government projects, etc., gives educated elites access to special privileges

            b. institutions of local, state, and national government organize polities in new configurations

            c. voting a new factor in local power relations

        4. Conflict and resistance

            a. caste and ethnic group organizations involved in various issues:

        1. survival of local traditions, especially language
        2. group uplift and access to special opportunities
    b. in a few areas, armed resistance movements against central state representatives
    c. little impact of environmental movements found in Himachal and Uttar Pradesh on the eastern region

V. Cultural Continuities

A. General lack of common cross-ethnic group culture traits
1. Role of inner frontiers separating settlers and abetting divergent patterns of socio-cultural evolution
2. Groups develop different cultural practices to accentuate their group boundaries

B. Tibeto-Burman Languages
1. Language often coterminous with recognized ethnic boundaries
2. Even distantly spoken dialects of the same ethnic language are not intelligible to other speakers; e.g. there are over 14 dialect versions of Rai

C. Indic languages are linguae francae in states and sub-regions where Tibeto-Burman peoples are numerically dominant
1. Gradual encapsulation of Tibeto-Burman speakers by Indic speakers
2. Examples:
    a. Nepali language in Nepal and areas of India and Bhutan settled by Nepalis
    b. Assamese in Arunachal Pradesh

D. Religious Traditions
1. Each ethnic group has developed its own pantheon, priesthood, ritualism
2. Buddhism
    a. some Tibeto-Burman peoples still preserve Tibetan Buddhism
        1. usually Nyingma-pa school
        2. villages marked by small monasteries, *lama* recruitment, *chorten, mani* walls
        3. Examples:
            a. Tamangs
            b. Gurungs
            c. Thakali
            d. Lepcha

        e. Upland Magar

        f. Newars

        g. Sunuwars

   b. Others have little indication of Buddhist influence

        1. Kham Magars

        2. Thami

        3. Rai

        4. Limbu

        5. Api Tani

        6. Dafla

        7. Miri

        8. Galong

   c. Theravada Buddhism found among the Khamptis of the far east is the result of Burmese influences

3. Hinduism

   a. land-owning temples are key institutions

   b. networks of Brahman families linked by kinship, priestly initiation, training, and religious observances

   c. worship of Vishnu, Shiva, Devi, Krishna

   d. performance of life-cycle rites in which a Brahman is required

   e. celebration of major festivals:

        1. *Dashara (Dasain)*

        2. *Diwali (Tihar)*

        3. *Holi*

        4. *Tij*

        5. *Mahasivaratri*

   f. sacrifice of *mithan* cattle and water buffaloes unique to many peoples of the eastern region

   g. importance of astrology

4. Local deity and spirit cults

   a. pantheon of local forest, river, etc. deities

   b. specialists

        1. *jhankris* (shamans)

        2. oracles

   c. involved in healing and protection

5. Ancestor cults maintained in family lineages, rooted in homeland region

   a. yearly rituals to honor clan ancestors

   b. some groups believe that ancestor spirits reside in a fixed abode

        1. Rai and Limbus in hearth stones that both men and women preserve in their dwellings

        2. Thakali retain bones in lineage tombs

6. Common karma belief among Hinduized and Tibetanized peoples, but conceptions of the soul vary by ethnic group

E. Cultural Processes and Continuities
1. Sanskritization -- the preeminance of Hindu tradition in India and Nepal has led to the spread of the cultural complex dominated by Brahmanical norms and ideas
2. Tibetanization -- the preeminance of Buddhist tradition in those areas under the influence of persisting Buddhist cultural centers, especially in certain Nepalese areas, Sikkim, and Bhutan
3. Nationalization
   a. integration into the Nepalese economic and political system
   b. integration into the Indian economic and political system
4. Christian missionaries scattered across the northeast
5. Ethnic group boundary maintenance
   a. Peoples often accent their ethnic group and locality boundaries by emphasizing distinctive indigenous traits and adopting unique combinations from the possibilities cited above
   b. sometimes customs are at odds with normative Hindu and/or Buddhist traditions and groups practice impression management with regard to outsiders
      1. Gurungs accentuate their status hierarchies by adopting caste ideology, yet simultaneously augment their support of Buddhist *lamas*
      2. Newar Buddhist elite adopt full set of Brahmanical *samskaras*, yet do so by supporting a *vajracarya* priesthood to perform them and articulate a separate non-Hindu identity
      3. Rai divide clans based upon their separate origins:
         a. Lhasa
         b. Benares
6. The post-1990 creation of the Rastriya Janamukti Party, a group seeking united political action by Tibeto-Burman peoples
7. Distinctive aspects of material culture
   a. dress styles, jewelry, and special foods are important ethnic group boundary markers
   b. Nepalese man's national dress:
      1. *topi* hat
      2. *daura-suruwal* ("pants-coat") attire for men

Recommended Readings and References

Allen, N.J. "Thulung Wedding: The Hinduisation of a Ritual Cycle in East Nepal," *L'Ethnographie* 83, 1987, 15-33.

Andors, Ellen. "The Rodighar and its Role in Gurung Society*," Contributions to Nepalese Society* 1 (2), 1974, 10-24.

Dahal, Dilli R. *An Ethnographic Study of Social Change among the Athpahariya Rais of Dhankuta.* Kathmandu: CENAS, 1985.

English, Richard. *Gorkhali and Kiranti: Political Economy in the Eastern Hills of Nepal.* New York: New School for Social Research Ph.D. Dissertation, 1982.

Fricke, Tom. "Marriage, Social Inequality, and Women's Contact with their Natal Families in Alliance Societies: Two Tamang Examples," *American Anthropologist* 95, 1993, 395-419.

Fürer-Haimendorf, Christoph von. *The Apa Tanis and Their Neighbors: A Primitive Civilization of the Eastern Himalayas.* New York: Free Press, 1962.

Gorer, Geoffrey. *Himalayan Village: An Account of the Lepchas of Sikkim* (2nd ed.) NY: Basic Books, 1967.

Holmberg, David H. *Order in Paradox: Myth, Ritual, amd Exchange among Nepal's Tamang.* Ithaca: Cornell University Press, 1989.

Kondinya. *Monastic Buddhism among the Khamtis of Arunachal.* New Delhi: National Publishing House, 1986.

McDougal, Charles. *The Kulunge Rai.* Kathmandu: Ratna Pustak Bhandar, 1979.

Manzardo, Andrew E. *To Be Kings of the North: Community, Adaptation and Impression Management in the Thakali of Western Nepal.* Ann Arbor: University Microfilms, 1978.

March, Kathryn S. "Weaving, Writing and Gender," *Man* (N.S.) 18, 1984, 729-744.

Messerschmidt, Donald A. "Ecological Change and Adaptation among the Gurungs of the Nepal Himalayas," *Human Ecology* 4 (2), 1976, 167-185.

_____. *The Gurungs of Nepal: Conflict and Change in a Village Society.* New Delhi: Oxford University Press, 1976.

Mumford, Stan Royal. *Himalayan Dialogue: Tibetan Lamas and Gurung Shamans in Nepal.* Madison: University of Wisconsin Press, 1989.

Peet, Robert Creighton. *Migration, Culture, and Community: A Case Study from Rural Nepal.* Ann Arbor: University Microfilms International, 1978.

Rai, Navin K. *People of the Stones: The Chepangs of Central Nepal.* Kathmandu: CENAS, 1985.

Rose, Leo and Fisher, Margaret W. *The Northeast Frontier Agency of India.* Washington DC: Department of State Publications (8288), 1967.

Siiger, Halfdan. *The Lepchas: Culture and Religion of a Himalayan People.* Copenhagen: The National Museum of Denmark, 1967.

_____. *Ethnological Field Research in Chitral, Sikkim, and Assam: Preliminary Report.* Copenhagen: Historik-filogogiske Meddeleslser udgivet af Det Kongelige Danske Videnskabernes Selskab, Bind 36 (2), 1956.

Tibetan Buddhist *Mani* Stone

Chapter 13

TIBETAN HIGHLANDS REGION

I. Physical Geography

A. Map location: high altitude region above 8,000 ft. on both sides of the high Himalayan peaks from Ladakh in the modern state of Jammu and Kashmir through Himachal Pradesh, Uttar Pradesh, Nepal, Sikkim, Bhutan; and across Arunachal Pradesh to the border with Burma

B. Recognized sub-areas (from west to east):
1. Ladakh, former independent kingdom called Maryul ("Low Country"), now part of the India.
2. Zanskar, former tributary of Ladakh, also part of modern India
3. Lahul-Spiti, region in Himachal Pradesh, north of Kulu
4. Guge, area once part of former central Himalayan Kingdom that existed from c. 900-1200 and was influential in Tibetan history; former capital at Tsaparang now deserted
5. Ngaris, area around the region dominated by Mt. Kailash and Lake Manasarovar
6. Humla, far northwestern region of Nepal
7. Dolpo, plateau of central Nepal on the Langu and upper Bheri watersheds, once closely linked to Mustang
8. Tichurong, valley east of Dolpo and west of Dhaulagiri
9. Mustang or Lo, border kingdom on the upper Gandaki
10. Manang, an upland valley east of the Annapurna range known for its modern traders
11. Nupri, highland area at the headwaters of the Buri Gandaki, northeast of Manaslu Himalaya
12. Langtang, region north of the Kathmandu Valley
13. Helambu, region northeast of the Kathmandu Valley
14. Solu-Khumbu, homeland of the Sherpas
15. Dingri, settlement founded by an Indian Buddhist teacher in the twelveth century, a stopping place on the old Kathmandu-Lhasa trade route;
16. Sikkim, former independent Tibetan kingdom, now part of India
17. Bhutan, the sole remaining independent Tibetan- origin state in the Himalayan region
18. Sherdukpen, region of Arunachal Pradesh

C. Topography
1. High mountains, upland valleys and plateaus linked to other areas by trails crossing high passes
2. Landforms shaped by heavy glaciation
3. Includes the tributaries of the Indus, Ganges, and Brahmaputra (Tib.: Tsang-po)

D. Climate
1. Area of extreme cold in winter, intense solar radiation, high winds, short growing season
2. Snowfall heaviest in the eastern regions
3. Western regions depend more on glacial melt than rain for water supplies

E. Flora & Fauna
1. Climate is so severe that tree line usually stops at 14,000 ft., and only specially adapted plants survive at higher elevations
2. Only specially adapted wild animals survive there: mountain goats, blue sheep, feral yaks, snow leopards
3. Forestation shrinking in western and central regions, but still prolific in the east

F. Communication networks follow very limited avenues of human passage: on trade routes, across accessible passes, and along new roads

II. Subsistance and Trade Patterns

A. Introduction
1. Ecological micro-environments dictate a wide spectrum of subsistence that varies according to altitude, daily sunlight, water, winds, and household resources
2. In most areas, people practice agro-pastoral trans-humance, mixing agricultural production, animal husbandry, and other means of earning a cash income
3. Forest resources of special importance
    a. firewood (In Solu-Khumbu, Nepal, estimated annual wood use is five tons per household)
    b. leaves, needles collected as fertillizer
    c. timber an essential building material
    d. groves owned by villages and monasteries often appoint watchmen
4. Household is the primary economic unit: basis for land-holding, production, taxation

Kanji Village, Ladakh

High Altitude Pastures above Namche Bazaar, Nepal

B. Nomadic Pastoralists
1. Few now survive in the region
2. Move with the seasons, survive off of their large flocks of sheep and yaks
   a. milk products and meat for consumption
   b. wool for clothing and movable dwellings
   c. sheep and yaks used for trade with settled people, especially to acquire grains, vegetables, luxury goods, etc.

C. Agricultural Production
1. Cropping patterns according to altitude and water resources:
   a. barley
   b. buckwheat
   c. winter wheat
   d. potatoes
   e. millet
2. Except for exceptional areas where the winters are mild, all crops are sown in the summer
3. In areas of little rainfall, total dependence on irrigation channeling glacial runoff
4. In some areas, labor shortages restrict production

D. Animal Husbandry
1. Symbiotic relationship between humans and animals absolutely essential to ecological adaptation
2. Domestic animals: yak, *dzo*, sheep, goats, dogs
3. Uses:
   a. plowing traction
   b. milk, meat products
   c. dung for fuel and fertilizer
   d. household heat when stabled on ground floor below human dwellings
   e. transport of trade goods
   f. skins for clothing, utensils
   g. dogs herd sheep and guard settlement
4. Sheep and goats more important in west; yaks and cattle more important in the east
5. General pattern: after sowing summer crops in main settlement, men drive their herds to highland pastures to coincide with peak grass and scrub growing season

E. Trade
1. Regional trade in salt/grain cycles and in woolen cloth produced by household weavers
2. Long distance trade in Indo-Tibetan luxuries

3. Chinese takeover in Tibet disrupted the former and ended the old patterns of caravan trading
4. Retail trade: penetration of Indian industrial goods into highland markets

F. Employment and Migration
1. Local labor exchanged for in-kind payment
2. Migration to middle hills and tarai as agricultural laborers in winter
3. "Subsistence trade": individuals travel and trade village goods (especially woolens) outside of the home area to avoid consuming limited foods available there and, if possible, to make a profit
4. Tourist industry a dramatic new source of income in a few areas: Solu-Khumbu, Helambu, Manang, Langtang

III. Settlement Patterns

A. Historical background
1. Middle Period consolidation of Tibetan empire that extended its frontiers out to most Himalayan highland regions and some mid-montane areas
2. Some Tibeto-Burman peoples were integrated into Tibetan polities especially through conversion to Buddhism and submission to monastic landlordism and rule
3. People from the Tibetan plateau also migrated into these areas, especially non-Gelugpa supporters, during and after the harsh measures of consolidation enacted by the Fifth Dalai Lama (1617-1682)
4. Some groups with cultural links to Tibet identify themselves using the Tibetan word "*Bod*;" others have adopted the word "*Bhotiya*" to refer to them; today, many Himalayan peoples regard this as a derogatory ethnonym
5. Great variation in highland settlements regarding the extent of "conversion" to Tibetan social organization, culture, preservation of local autonomy
6. The Shah conquest (1769) and subsequent efforts to keep Kathmandu dominant in Tibetan trade through Nepal hindered many highland trade economies
7. Chinese takeover of traditional Tibet overturned the political and cultural relationships that once linked the Himalayan highlands to central Tibet

B. Village settlements
1. Some of the highest human habitations in the world are located in this region
2. Usually small and nucleated, resembling "mountain oases" in difficult terrain

Vegetable Seller, Ladakh

Buddhist Monastery and Mani Wall, Upper Kali Gandaki Region

3. Located in places having natural advantages
    a. free from avalanche danger
    b. ready water supply
    c. along reliable trade routes
    d. access to good upland pastures
    e. natural defensive landforms
4. Often families have multiple dwellings:
    a. highland structures for summer shepherding
    b. year-round central site(s) for agriculture
5. Villages marked by entrance gates, small monasteries (*gompas*) and shrines (*mani* walls, *chortens*, etc.)
6. Sometimes there are separate villages for low status artisans and recent Tibetan refugees
7. Stone houses with slate roofs, wooden support beams, and small windows

C. Political and Commercial Centers

1. *Dzong*: monasteries that became the dominant religious, administrative, and commercial centers of their regions
2. Major towns:
    a. Leh, former capital of the Ladakh Kingdom and major trade center;
    b. Hemis, one of the largest monasteries of the region, built and maintained by the Drukpa sect of Bhutan;
    c. Keylong, dominant market town on upper Chandra river along Himachal Pradesh - Zanskar trade route
    d. Spiti, gateway town on route to Ladakh
    e. Manali, crossroad town in upper Himachal Pradesh
    f. Tsaparang, the now deserted former capital of the old Guge kingdom
    g. Purang, trade center in highland Uttar Pradesh
    h. Simikot, capital of the Humla district of Nepal
    i. Mugu, main town of a highland valley east of Humla
    j. Tibrikot, chief city of Dolpo
    k. Mustang, capital of the Mustang kingdom now on the Tibetan-Nepalese border
    l. Kirong, important settlement on the old Kathmandu-Lhasa route
    m. Namche Bazaar, chief market town in the Sherpa region
    n. Walongchung, chief bazaar town on a formerly important trade route in eastern Nepal
    o. Gangtok, formerly capital of independent Sikkim and site of important Karmapa sect monastery, Rumtek *gompa*
    p. Paro, important town of western Bhutan
    q. Thimpu, capital of modern Bhutan
    r. Tashigang, major *dzong* of eastern Bhutan
    s. Tawang, the town in Arunachal Pradesh to which the Dalai Lama fled in 1959

3. Tibetan Refugees dispersed across the Himalayan region:
    a. monasteries and major settlements:
        1. Jammu and Kashmir: Leh, Choklamsar
        2. Himachal Pradesh: Dharamsala, Manali, Dalhousie, Tashi Jong, Rewalsar, Satsun, Chauntra Bir
        3. Uttar Pradesh: Lingtsang, Herbertpur, Clement Town, Mussoorie, Simla, Dolanji
        4. Nepal: Dhorpatan, Pokhara, Mustang, Kathmandu, Solu Khumbu, Walung
        5. West Bengal: Darjeeling, Ghum, Sonada, Kalimpong
        6. Sikkim: Gangtok, Kunphel
        7. Bhutan
        8. Arunachal Pradesh: Tawang, Tenzingang, Tezu, Miao
    b. Refugee community may not engage in "political" activities

D. Pilgrimage centers
    1. Prestigious monasteries where revered *lamas*, saints, and shrines are located
    2. Almost every region has a cave, natural formation, or shrine associated with a great Buddhist *lama*, especially Padmasambhava and Milarepa
    3. Important Sites:
        a. Mt. Kailash, identified as the central mountain of the world in traditional cosmology
        b. Lake Manosarovar, immense lake on the Tibetan plateau
        c. Muktinath, a sacred complex on the Gandaki River
        d. Kathmandu Valley sites
            1. Svayambhu
            2. Bauddha
        e. Hajo, submontane site; in the Tibetan tradition identified with Kushinara, the death place of the Buddha

IV. Social Relations

A. Ethnic Groups (See Map 9)
1. Tibetan ethnicity varies from west to east, linked to geographic homeland, marked by dialect differences
2. Migrants from other places in the highlands, especially central Tibet, adds to the social complexity
3. Three general types of people recognized in Tibetan parlance:
    a. Nomads
    b. Mixed agriculturalists
    c. Traders

B. Social Organization
1. Castes and ethnic groups typically divided into named sub-divisions associated with specific localities
2. Local hierarchies based upon endogamous caste groups
    a. Percentages of population in greater Tibet in the early modern period: [Gompo 1984]
        1. Clergy 2%
        2. Nobles 1%
        3. Taxpaying Commoners (*tre-ba*) 40%
            a. landowning agriculturalists
            b. merchants
        4. Small householders (dujung) 50%
            a. mostly landless
            b. worked as laborers
        5. Former slaves [in some areas]
        6. Low artisans 7%
            a. blacksmiths
            b. cobblers
            c. tailors
    b. For Ladakh
        1. *rgyal-rigs*- "royalty"
        2. *sku-drag*- "nobility"
        3. *dmans-rigs*- "commoners"
        4. *rigs-nan*- "mean class"
        5. blacksmiths, carpenters, musicians
    c. For Dolpo
        1. *gzi-mi* - "men of the place", regarded as the original settlers
        2. *phyogs-mi* - "those of the outlands", later arrivals
        3. *gar-ra* - "low artisans"
        4. *ba-ra* - "men without lineages", recent arrivals
3. Constraints on population growth
    a. polyandry limits divisibility of family estates
    b. norm of placing one son in the monastery limits marriage partners
    c. delaying marriage of daughter to retain her labor
    d. monastic life for women as *anis* ("homeless")
4. Tibetan societes emphasize the purity of the patrilineage, which is expressed commonly by the concept of "passing on the bone" of the father to his offspring
5. Tibetan women
    a. the least restricted and most independent of all Himalayan peoples
    b. wide overlap in male/female work tasks

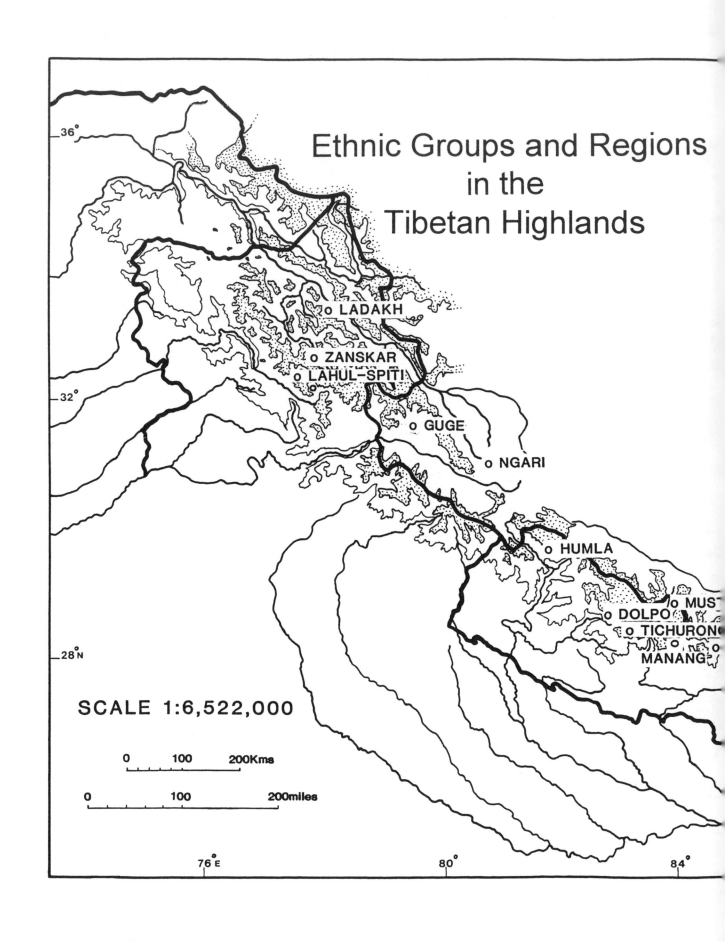

Ethnic Groups and Regions
in the
Tibetan Highlands

o LADAKH

o ZANSKAR
o LAHUL–SPITI

o GUGE

o NGARI

o HUMLA

o MUST

o DOLPO

o TICHURON

MANANG

SCALE 1:6,522,000

0   100   200Kms

0   100   200miles

36°

32°

28°N

76° E

80°

84°

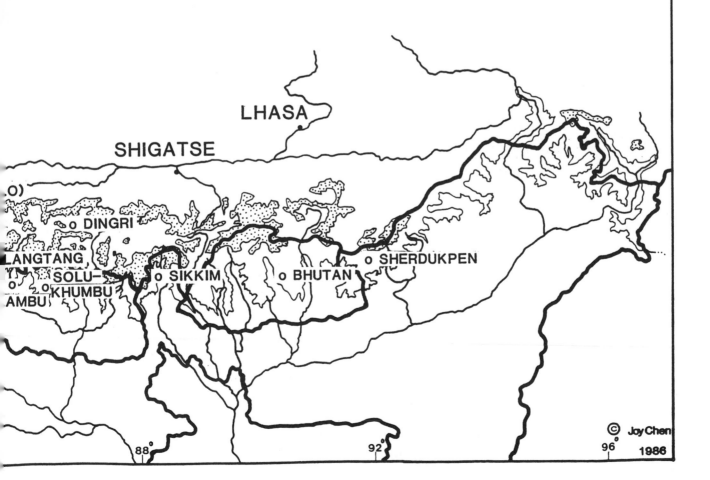

9

feet   meters

16,404 ⟩ 5000
Highlands
8,202 ⟩ 2500

LHASA

SHIGATSE

O)

o DINGRI

LANGTANG

SOLU-   o SIKKIM   o BHUTAN   o SHERDUKPEN

KHUMBU

AMBU

© Joy Chen

88°   92°   96°   1986

6. Kinship system
    a. patrilineal, clan exogamy, and virilocal marriage
    b. polyandry practiced, usually by an upper caste minority
    c. divorce more tolerated than other areas
7. Because grazing resources are limited, special institutions commonly regulate pasture rotation and the separate seasonal movements of herds
8. Institution of forest guards appointed by village council or monastic owners
9. Norm of village solidarity and mutual aid

C. Political Relations

1. Dominant groups
    a. landowning monasteries
    b. descendents of former local nobility
    c. new political aspirants
    d. wealthy merchants
2. Rivalries among Buddhist sects reflect nobility factions and their separate alliances with major monasteries
3. Processes of social dominance
    a. Tibetanization
        1. submission to local and/or sect's monastic authorities
        2. missionizing by lamas
    b. Sanskritization
        1. trade strategies have led some Tibetans to political conciliation with caste Hindus, especially among Kumaoni Tibetans, Humlis, Sherpas
        2. many have claimed *Rajput* caste status and geneologies
4. Political Articulation
    a. In the Tibetan Autonomous Zone of the People's Republic of China, Chinese law and officials dominate
    b. Other regions have been incorporated into states in which Tibetan peoples are a minority:
        1. Jammu and Kashmir
        2. Himachal Pradesh
        3. Uttar Pradesh
        4. Nepal
        5. Sikkim
        6. Aruncahal Pradesh
    c. For the Tibetan refugee community, governmental organizations and international institutions centered in Dharamsala seek to preserve Tibetan culture, work for the best interests of the Tibetan people, and the return of the Dalai Lama to Tibet
    d. Only in Bhutan does autonomous internal rule prevail, although India controls Bhutan's external affairs

5. Conflict and resistance
    a. prejudice against Tibetans among high caste groups
    b. competition for resources between recent refugees and already settled Tibetan peoples

V. Cultural Continuities

A. Languages

1. Dardic speaking Tibetans of western Ladakh
2. Dialects of Tibetan conform to regional identities; major examples:
    a. Ladakhi (India)
    b. Humli (Nepal)
    c. Langthang
    d. Sherpa
    e. Dzong-kha (Bhutan)
3. Central Tibetan can usually be understood by the literate and so constitutes a lingua franca in many areas

B. Religious Traditions

1. Indigenous Tibetan Division of Religious traditions:
    a. *lha-chos*: "divine law", i.e. Buddhism
    b. *bon-chos*: Bon
    c. *mi-chos*: "law of mankind", i.e. folk religion
2. Buddhism
    a. Major Buddhist sects:
        1. Nyingmapa
        2. Gelugpa
        3. Kargypa
            a. Drukpa of Bhutan
            b. Karmapa of Sikkim
        4. Sakyapa
    b. Types of lamas
        1. learned heads of the major schools who have recognized reincarnations (*tulku*); these figures visit the hinterlands periodically to heal and teach
        2. accomplished scholars (*geshe*)
        3. abbots of major regional monasteries
        4. celibate monastics of major monasteries
        5. local married lamas who undergo monastic residence and training in their youth (usually 3 years), wear special clothing upon resumption of lay life, and who continue to perform rituals and practice meditation in their villages
        6. oracle lamas attached to great monasteries

     c. Types of Buddhist monasteries (*gompas*)
        1. seats of the major schools with thousands of lamas in Ladakh and Bhutan; former sites in central Tibet now located in Himalayan periphery, e.g. Dharamsala
        2. important regional *dzongs* with fifty inmates
        3. small village establishments with a few monks
     d. Major Rituals: lama-laymen relations
        1. masked dancing festivals: lamas act out the important mythological accounts of Buddhist saints conquering local demons and establishing the tradition
            a. *mani rimdu* re-enacts Padmasambhava's conquest of the Bon priests
        2. exorcistic healing rituals
        3. propitiation rituals
        4. climate control: *pujas* for securing rainfall and preventing hailstorms a major concern of highland agriculturalists
        5. thread-cross "evil spirit catchers" (*mDos*) placed on buildings
        6. lamas name children
        7. death rites: body dismembered in remote location by low caste specialists and fed to birds of prey
        8. ascetic retreats for laymen (*nyunge*)
3. Bon Tradition
     a. roots in ancient Tibet, especially in the western region
     b. throughout history, gradual imitation of Buddhist cosmology, pantheon, meditation, monasticism, ritualism, but with reversals in practice
     c. animal sacrifice key contrast with Buddhist rituals
     d. stronghold regions: Dolpo, upper Arun Valley, Nepal
4. Independent spirit cults
     a. oracles
     b. shamans
5. Folk Pantheon
     a. *lu*: (Skt: *naga*) spirits of the earth and water sources
     b. *gNyan*: spirits of trees and rocks
     c. demons in the form of savage huntsmen, led by king, *rtsu*
     d. tent protectors
     e. divinity of the hearth
     f. *dGra-lha*: the "foe god" who protects a person against his/her enemies
6. Karma belief and the ethos of merit making
7. Resort to astrological calculations common for all Tibetan peoples
8. Folklore recounting exploits of the Yeti, a fabulous mountain being, a giant with human features

D. Cultural Processes and Continuities
  1. Tibetanization
     a. trends toward high Tibetan orthodoxy, especially in adopting orthodox cultural agenda from central Tibet
        1. in festival celebrations
        2. ending animal sacrifices
     b. introduced recently in some areas by refugee lamas
     c. Dalai Lama and other high lamas as symbols of cultural unity
     d. general lack of pan-regional Tibetan solidarity
  2. Sanskritization
     a. in many areas, Tibetan peoples have been integrated into caste society (e.g. Johar Valley, Uttar Pradesh)
     b. adoption of Hindu calendar and major festival observances (Dasain, Tihar), Brahmanical rituals, and Rajput role models
     c. decline of polyandry
  3. Nationalization
     a. integration into modern states and tensions with older political systems
     b. in Bhutan, analogous to Sanskritization in Hindu states: adoption of state-supported Buddhist practices
     c. In parts of India, some Tibetan groups have claimed "scheduled caste" to gain access to special state aid programs
  4. Distinctive Aspects of Material Culture
     a. Woolen clothing common, but styles reflect regional and ethnic boundaries
        1. Men's *gho* in Bhutan
        2. Woman's headdresses
     b. Millet beer and distilled spirits
     c. Barley flour (*tsampa*), a staple of the diet
        1. added to tea
        2. used for noodles to make *thukpa*, meat noodle soup
        3. toasted and eaten as snack
     d. Hot buttered tea made in a churn
     e. Hard yak cheese
     f. Prayer wheels and prayer flags

Recommended Readings and References

Brower, Barbara. *Sherpa of Khumbu: People, Livestock, and Landscape*. Delhi: Oxford University Press, 1991.

Dargyay, Eva K. "Buddhism in Adaptation: Ancestor gods and their Tantric Counterparts in the Religious Life of Zanskar," *History of Religion* 28, 1988, 123-134.

Erdman, Ferry. "Social Stratification in Ladakh," in *Recent Research on Ladakh*. Munich: Weltforum-Verlag, 1983.

Fisher, James F. *Trans-Himalayan Traders: Economy, Society, and Culture in Northwest Nepal*. Berkeley: University of California Press, 1986.

Gombo, Ugen. "Cultural Expressions of Social Stratification in Traditional Tibet: Caste and Casteism in Traditional Tibetan Society," *Anthropology* VII, 1982, 43-72.

Grimshaw, Anna. *Servants of the Buddha: Winter in a Himalayan Convent*. Cleveland: The Pilgrim Press, 1994.

Jest, Corneille. *Dolpo: Communautes de Langue Tibetaine du Nepal*. Paris: Editions du CNRS, 1975.

Jackson, David P. *The Mollas of Mustang: Historical, Religious and Oratorical Traditions of the Nepalese-Tibetan Borderland*. Dharamsala: Library of Tibetan Works and Archives, 1984.

Kleinert, Christian. "Dolpo: The Highest Settlement in Western Nepal," *Journal of the Nepal Research Centre* 1, 1977, 11-24.

Kvaerne, Per. "Continuity and Change in Tibetan Monasticism," in Chai-Shin Yu ed. *Korean and Asian Religious Systems*. Toronto: University of Toronto Press, 1977, 83-98.

Levine, Nancy E. *The Dynamics of Polyandry: Kinship, Domesticity, and Population on the Tibetan Border*. The University of Chicago Press, 1988.

_____. "Opposition and Interdependence: Demographic and Economic Perspectives on Nyimba Slavery," in James L. Watson ed. *Asian and African Systems of Slavery*. Berkeley: University of California Press, 1980, 195-222.

Neeru, Nandam. *Tawang: Land of the Mon*. New Delhi: Vikas, 1982.

Ortner, Sherry B. *Sherpas Throught their Rituals*. Cambridge University Press, 1978.

_____. *High Religion: A Cultural and Political History of Sherpa Buddhism*. Princeton University Press, 1989.

Ramble, Charles. "Rule by Play in Southern Mustang," in Charles Ramble and Martin Brauen, eds. *Anthropology of Tibet and the Himalayas* Zurich: Volkerkundemuseum, 1993, 287-301.

Samuel, Geoffrey. *Civilized Shamans: Buddhism in Tibetan Societies*. Washington DC: Smithsonian Institution Press,.1993.

Stevens, Stanley F. *Claiming the High Ground*. Berkeley: University of California Press, 1992.

Vohra, Rohit. "Ethnographic Notes on the Buddhist Dards of Ladakh: The Brog-pa," *Zeitschrift fur Ethnologie* 107 (1), 1982, 69-94.

Tibetan Lama

Stok Palace, Ladakh

PART IV:

MAJOR CULTURAL CENTERS

Southern Entrance to the Kashmir Valley

Chapter 14

KASHMIR VALLEY REGION

I. Physical Geography (See Map 10)

A. Map location: large oval valley in Indian state of Jammu and Kashmir 85 miles long and 25 miles wide at an average altitude of 6,000 ft.

B. Topography
   1. Pir Panjal range on the west and Shivalekh hills on the east demarcate Valley
   2. Dominated by undulating hills, rivers, and glacial lakes
   3. Watershed
      a. Jhelum river, tributary of the Indus, flows northwest and west into the plains of Pakistan
      b. major lakes: Wuler, Haigam, Anchar, Dal

C. Climate
   1. Temperate climate, with chilly winters, a mild hot season, and moderate summer monsoon
   2. Period of winter monsoon rainfall and occasional light snowfall
   3. Area noted throughout India for being a mountain paradise

D. Flora and Fauna
   1. Forest tracts of deodar, firs, and pine survive only in isolated stands and along upland periphery
   2. Upland pastures
   3. Wild animals in highlands include sheep, bears, wildcats, monkeys now largely confined to game preserves

E. Communication Networks
   1. Local: lakes connected by rivers and canals make boat transport an important feature
   2. Passes to Tibet
      a. Zogi La
   3. Passes to India
      a. Baramula, in northwest
      b. Banihal pass, to the south
   4. Direct airlinks links to plains, to Leh (Ladakh)

F. 1991 Population of the State of Jammu and Kashmir: 7,718,700

II. Subsistence and Trade Patterns

A. Agricultural production
1. Over half the valley population subsists primarily on agriculture
2. Irrigation on lowlands that support intensive rice cultivation and multi-cropped vegetables
3. Dry rice and corn on non-irrigated upland terraces
4. Cash crops
   a. fruits
   b. saffron
   c. silkworm trees

B. Animal husbandry
1. Gujjar herders in upland areas
2. Silkworm breeding
3. Cows, water buffalos, in some places fed lake vegetation as fodder

C. Trade
1. Local networks
   a. in staple grains and foods produced in the Valley and nearby hills
   b. retail business in locally produced and plains consumer goods
   c. herder-agriculturalist exchanges in villages: dairy products for grain
2. Tourism entrepreneurs
3. Export economy, especially in woolens and carpets

D. Industrial Production
1. Small-scale cottage industries provide wage labor
   a. woven cloth, especially wool and silk
   b. metalwork
   c. artisans working in wood and stone carving
   d. embroidered and knitted clothing
   e. silk and wool carpets
   f. leatherwork
   g. tourist sale items
2. Factories

E. Other wage labor
1. Seasonal agriculture
2. Tourist industry
3. Employment in government, army, schools

KASHMIR VALLEY

10

© Joy Chen
1986

Leh

Kargi

Burzil Pass

Zoji Pass

Sonamarg

Amarnath Cave

Pahlgam

Anantnag

Jammu

Wular Lake

Dal Lake

Baramula

Srinagar

Gulmarg

Pir Panjal Pass

Muzaffarabad

Jhelam

Road
River, Lake
Valley
Major Town
Pass

SCALE

0   10   20 miles

74°E

75°

76°

35°

34°N

III. Settlement Patterns

A. Historical background

1. Long history of groups migrating into the Valley
2. Kashmir civilization centered in river basins and on intensive rice cultivation
3. Hindu-Buddhist civilization transformed to Muslim dominance by middle of fifteenth century
4. Incorporation into Mughal empire in 1589
5. Sikh rule (1846-1947) a product of British imperial policy and expediency, favored Hindu elite, the *brahman* pandits, who became dominant in many rural areas
6. Local *maharaja* forbade British from owning land or building, so in 1888, first houseboats were built; now the most important domiciles for tourists
7. Abolition of large landed estates in 1950, the most radical land reform in the subcontinent
8. Indo-Pakistan Wars over Indian ownership of Kashmir:
   a. 1947-1949
   b. 1965
   c. 1986-1994: continuing border skirmishes
9. In rural areas, continuing evolution of Hindu-Muslim synthesis and interaction

B. Village settlements

1. General tendency to find villages in well-watered areas, near lands suitable for intensive agriculture
2. 60 % of villages are Muslim
3. Average size of village is 500 people
4. Gujjar herders tend to live in upland forested areas

C. Political & Commercial centers

1. Major towns:
   a. Srinagar, the largest city with ancient roots, focal point of regional political life, industry, and tourism
   b. Gulmarg, fashionable hill station with winter skiing, also called "Meadow of Wildflowers"
   c. Pahalgam, until recently a small Gujjar village, now a tourist center
   d. Baramula, a gateway community located where the Jhelum river exits the Valley
   e. Sonmarg, major settlement on the road to Kargil
2. Landowning elites and middlemen dominate local production, marketing, and politics
3. Every ethnic group represented in politics, bureaucracy, and in business

184

D. Pilgrimage centers in the Kashmir Valley
   1. For centuries, religious elites have set up shrines across the landscape to resemble shrines in India
   2. Hindu
       a. Shankaracarya Hill
       b. Hari Parvat
       c. Amarnath cave
       d. Anantanag
   3. Muslim
       a. Shah Hamdam Mosque, Srinagar
       b. Bawan

IV. Social Relations

A. Ethnic Groups Populations (1975 estimate)
   1. Muslims- 95 %
       a. "indigenous groups"- 65 %
       b. immigrants still retaining pre-migration identity- 35 %
           1. Arabs
           2. Pathans
           3. Gujjar
           4. Bakarwal
   2. Hindus- 5%
       a. indigenous *Bhatta Brahmans*
           1. also known by term "*pandit*"
           2. claim *Saraswat Brahman* sub-caste status
           3. recall group history to time of Sikander, dividing community into two sections:
               a. those who fled persecutions and returned
               b. those who remained
           4. study of Persian enabled them to work as officials in Muslim courts
           5. two endagamous marriage circles (*gotras*)
               a. *Gor*: ritualists, Sanskrit scholars
               b. *Ka:rkun:* "Persian court officials"
       b. Kashmiri *Vaishyas*: "*Buher*"
           1. grocers and confectioners in Srinagar
           2. now claim "*Pandit*" status
       c. Immigrant Hindus

B. Social Organization
   1. Castes and ethnic groups typically divided into named sub-divisions associated with specific localities
   2. Two separate social orders, Brahmanical and Islamic, in subjective view of Hindus and Muslims

3. Muslim Society
    a. kinship system is North Indian
        1. patrilineal descent
        2. formal male dominance with strong filiofocal bonds
        3. exception: parallel cross-cousin marriage practiced
    b. groups:
        1. *Zamindar* (2/3): landowner-cultivators
        2. *Nangair* (1/3): occupational groups that are mostly landless
        3. *Ulama* and Sufi *sheikhs*
    c. hierarchies:
        1. groups regarded as *zats*, "separate geneological lineages"
        2. ranking:
            a. *Sayyids*, descendants of Ali, regarded as the most prestigious because of their early conversion to Islam
            b. Pathans, migrants from the Hindu Kush
            c. Mughals, descendants from the rulers of India
            d. Gujjars, herders
            e. lowest Nangair groups, the Dom and Vaitals, are only *zats* which cannot inter-dine with other Muslim groups

4. Hindu Society
    a. pollution-purity observant Brahmanical caste
    b. lacking lower castes, *pandits* must rely on Muslim workers, the *Nangair*, to perform services that would demean their Brahmanical status
    c. Brahman ritualists (*Gor*) as key figures and regarded as somewhat superior

C. Political Relations

1. Dominant groups
    a. *Pandits* had superior standing in rural Kashmir during Dogra rule; still retain economic power and prestige in rural areas
    b. Muslim families with histories of political activity
    c. Wealthy merchants and businessmen in Srinagar
2. Processes of social dominance
    a. Islamization
        1. conformity to orthodoxy basis for social standing and political interaction
        2. institutional activities at mosques
            a. political organization
            b. Friday prayers often the occasion for mass meetings

Mosque in Downtown Srinagar

3. attitudes toward Hindus:
     a. non-believers (*kafirs*)
     b. no inter-dining
     c. lack of pollution-purity observances in
        household access and marriage
4. converted Hindus are usually welcomed, but treated as
  social inferiors

187

   b. birth status as basis for social ranking common for all groups

   c. for Gujjars, tribal council (*jirga*) is chief social institution

  3. Political articulation

   a. movements to deny Pandits services in rural areas

   b. political party formation on ethnic lines

  4. Hindu-Muslim relations

   a. different clothing

   b. later Muslim immigrants speak non-Kashmiri languages

   c. most Muslims have names common to the Islamic world

   d. overlapping but separate social orders:

    1. no inter-dining or *hookah* smoking between groups

    2. Pandits see all Muslims as ritually impure

    3. different forms of greeting:

     a. Hindu: "*Namaskar*"

     b. Muslim: "*Salam*"

    4. distinctive Hindu traits:

     a. clothing

     b. *tyok*, ritual mark on the forehead

     c. men's hair tuft

     d. sacred thread

   e. Since 1990, polarization, fratricide, Hindu exodus

V. Cultural Continuities

A. Major Language

  1. Kashmiri

   a. Sanskritized

   b. Persianized

  2. Hindu-Urdu in national political discourse and among immigrants

B. Religious Tradition

  1. Islam

   a. self-definition of individual key act of faith and indicator

   b. faith in *Koran*

   c. belief in one-ness of Allah and Mohammed as his prophet

   d. prayers at appointed times (*nimaz*)

   e. almsgiving (*zakat*)

   f. keeps *Ramazan*, holy month of restricted eating

   g. pilgrimage to Mecca (*hajj*)

   h. accepts the *kalimah* as recitation for an individual who seeks forgiveness of an "unwilling transgression": "Allah is but one and Mohammed is his Prophet."

   i. distinctions between Muslim schools and high philosophical terms of relevance only to literati

2. Hinduism
   a. key domains of organization: temple institutions and *Brahman* networks
   b. emphasis on *bhakti* faith to pantheon: Shiva-Pashupati, Vishnu, Ganesh, Devi, Krishna, Bhairav, Skanda, Indra
   c. Brahmanical rituals
      1. life cycle rites (*samskaras*)
      2. *homa pujas*
      3. *pinda* offerings to ancestors
   d. unique Pandit custom of religious specialization: daughter's sons study Sanskrit and become ritual specialists for community

Dal Lake, Srinagar, 1981

e. special festivals and observances
1. *herath*, a fifteen day celebration in Phalgun, during which families make special offerings to Shiva
2. goat sacrifices to female goddesses
3. little emphasis on vegetarianism
4. worship of patron goddesses Sarika and Rajna
f. lack of tantric elements
3. Mutual religious regard for "divine madmen" thought to be clairvoyant and empowered to both curse and bless others

C. Cultural Processes and Continuities
1. Islamization
a. strong influence through Persian language on all groups
b. conversion to Islam among *pandits*
c. Muslim community (*umma*) sees itself as separate from non-believers (*kafirs*)
2. Sanskritization
a. observance of high caste norms by *pandits* as marker of group's social boundaries
b. recent loss of respect by patrons for *pandit* priests undermines process
3. Nationalization
a. employment of Hindus in state dominated by elite Muslim families
b. development of loyalty to state of Kashmir among citizenry, with competing pulls toward India and Pakistan
4. Militant Islamization and Secessionism, 1989-

Recommended Readings and References

Asia Watch. *Kashmir Under Siege*. New York, 1992.

Barth, Frederik. "Ecological Relationships of Ethnic Groups in Swat, North Pakistan," *American Anthropologist* 58, 1956, 1083-1089.

Madan, T.N. "Religious Ideology in a Plural Society: the Muslims and Hindus of Kashmir," *Contributions to Indian Sociology* 6, 1972, 106-141.

_____. "Herath: A Religious Ritual and Its Secular Aspect," in L.P. Vidyarth ed. *Aspects of Religion in Indian Society*. New Delhi, 1977.

Kadian, Rajesh. *The Kashmir Tangle: Issues and Options*. Boulder: Westview Press, 1993.

Road to Sonmarg, Upper Kashmir Valley

Aerial View of Kathmandu, with the Hanuman Dhoka Palace

Chapter 15

KATHMANDU VALLEY REGION

I. Physical Geography (See Map 11)

    A. Map location

        1. A slightly elliptical bowl 20 miles in diameter, 4,600 ft. above sea level

        2. The capital of the modern state of Nepal

        3. Culture region extends to Nuvakot (north) and the Banepa Valley (east)

    B. Topography

        1. Defined by series of peaks and ridges between 7,000- 10,000 ft.

        2. Watershed

            a. Bagmati river, a tributary of the Ganges

            b. other major rivers:

                1. Vishnumati

                2. Hanumante

                3. Dhobi Khola

                4. Manohara

        3. Topsoil especially deep and rich

    C. Climate

        1. Temperate, with mild winters, mild summers

        2. Reliable monsoon season, when slightly over half the yearly rain falls

        3. Snowfall especially rare

        4. Air pollution in recent years

    D. Flora and fauna

        1. Forests survive only in religious and royal preserves

        2. Bamboo groves in scattered spots, especially at periphery

        3. Wild animals only in preserves and at periphery: monkeys, wildcats, wild boar, leopards

    E. Communication networks

        1. Passes to Tibet

            a. to north: via Nuwakot and Kuti

            b. to northeast: Kodari, now motorable

        2. Passes to India

            a. first motorable road through Hetauda and India, the Tribhuvan Rajpath, completed in 1956

            b. road to Pokhara and Butwal

            c. road to Narayanghat

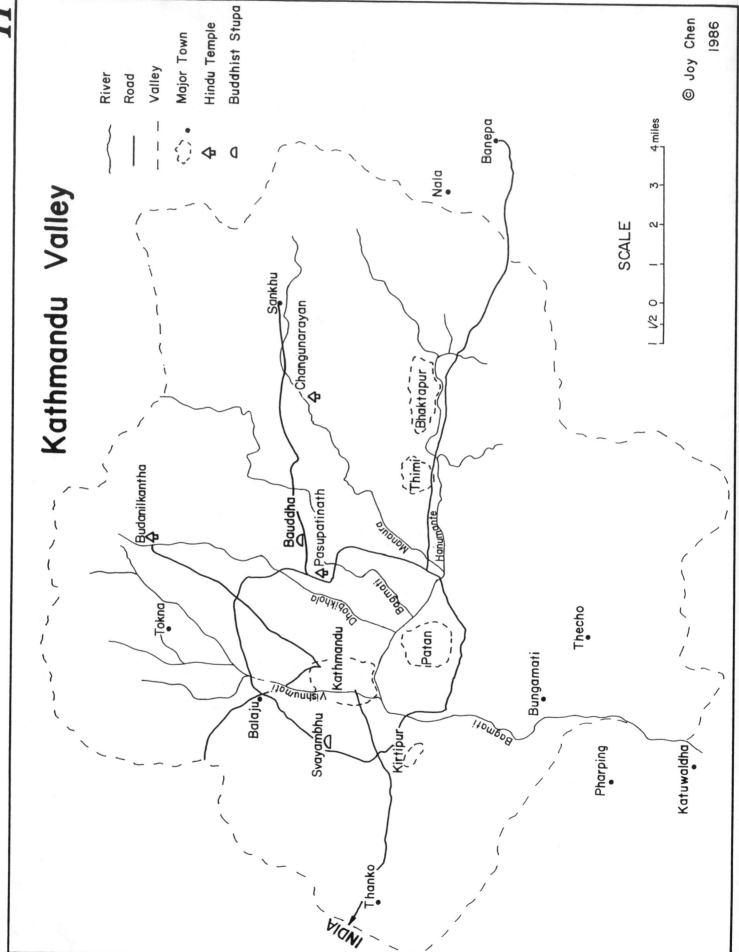

Kathmandu Valley

11

© Joy Chen 1986

Legend:
- River
- Road
- Valley
- Major Town •
- Hindu Temple
- Buddhist Stupa

SCALE

½ 0 1 2 3 4 miles

Towns and places: Budanilkantha, Tokna, Balaju, Svayambhu, Sankhu, Changunarayan, Bauddha, Pasupatinath, Kathmandu, Patan, Kirtipur, Thanko, Thimi, Bhaktapur, Nala, Banepa, Bungamati, Thecho, Pharping, Katuwaldha

Rivers: Vishnumati, Dhobikhola, Bagmati, Manoura, Hanumante, Bagmati

INDIA

3. Numerous footpaths leading to adjacent areas
4. Linked to every major town in the modern state by propeller aircraft
5. Linked to India, Bangladesh, Bhutan, Burma, Thailand, Singapore, Pakistan, Hong Kong, Dubai, Frankfurt, London by direct jet air service
6. During heavy monsoon season, all roads susceptible to landslides

II. Subsistence and Trade Patterns

A. Agricultural production
1. Over half the valley population subsists primarily on agriculture
2. Irrigation on lowlands that support intensive rice cultivation and multi-cropped vegetables
3. Dry rice, corn, and mustard on non-irrigated upland terraces

B. Animal husbandry
1. Little use of draught animals, a curious local feature: most land turned over by the hand hoe
2. Female water buffaloes kept for milk production and dung
3. Goats and sheep kept for meat, mostly in peripheral areas

C. Trade
1. Supports a large business class located in the largest cities
2. Local networks
   a. in staple grains and foods produced in the Valley and nearby hills
   b. in specialist production of consumer goods
      1. metalwork
      2. cloth
      3. clay products
      4. straw products
3. Import-export economy
   a. road-based trade with India and Tibet
   b. air-linked trade to SE Asia and beyond
   c. "second economy" involved in smuggling, etc., especially to India
4. Tourist industry has enhanced the Valley's prosperity further

D. Industrial Production
1. Small-scale cottage industries provide wage labor
   a. metalwork
   b. artisans working in wood and stone carving
   c. woven cloth
   d. sewn and knitted clothing
   e. tourist sale items

195

2. Factories
   a. modern plastics and glassware
   b. beer
   c. furniture
   d. cement
   e. brick making

E. Local wage labor for services
   1. Seasonal agriculture
   2. Tourist industry
   3. Employment in international agencies, in embassies

III. Settlement Patterns

A. Historical background
   1. Long history of groups migrating into the Valley
   2. Evolution of dominant society united by a common language, kinship exchanges, and locality ties
   3. Major Malla era cities in changing factional alliances; elites dominated the peasant agriculturalists
   4. After Shah conquest, Pahari elites take over political rule and provide entrance to new wave of Pahari migration into the region
   5. Rana period (1846-1950), an era of despotic rule: Rana families built Italian-style palaces, anti-Newar activities
   6. Influx of Tibetan refugees after 1959
   7. All factors have led to highly factionalized Newar society and great ethnic diversity in the capital

B. Village settlements:
   1. Newars (50 %)
      a. distinctive urban villages in lower river valleys and along hilltops arranged in a compact fashion
      b. tend to own best irrigated land
   2. Others in scattered separate settlements, often in upland sites:
      a. Parbatiyas (34%)
      b. Tamangs (10 %)
      c. Others 5%
   3. Tibetans (1 %) in refugee settlements

C. Political & Commercial centers
   1. Major Newar cities that were separate "countries" remain as key business centers:
      a. Kathmandu
      b. Patan
      c. Bhaktapur

        d. Dhulikhel

        e. Banepa

        f. Nuvakot

        g. Panauti

   2. Landowning elites and middlemen merchants dominate local production, marketing, and politics

   3. Kathmandu's dominance

        a. direct access to road link to India and as center for tourism and new international trade:

        b. new commercial centers

            1. New Road

            2. Naya Bazaar

            3. Bagh Bazaar

            4. Kalimati

   4. Greater Kathmandu as capital and international city

        a. elite among Nepal's many ethnic groups present

            1. politicians

            2. businessmen

            3. bureaucrats

        b. extensive contact with foreigners

            1. tourism

            2. foreign aid and embassies

   5. Valley as center of medical treatment by traditional ayurvedic and western-style practitioners

D. Pilgrimage Centers in the Kathmandu Valley

   1. For centuries, religious elites have set up shrines across the landscape to resemble shrines in India

   2. Peoples from the neighboring hill regions include deities of the great Valley shrines in their pantheons

   3. Hindu

        a. all-India Hinduism:

            1. Pashupati

            2. Budha Nilkantha

        b. other sites known to local Hindus

            1. Four Ganeshas

            2. Godavari

            3. Gokarna

            4. Changu Narayan

            5. Dakshin Kali

            6. Gosainkund, in the highlands north of the Valley

4. Buddhist
   a. Buddhist sites:
      1. Svayambhu
      2. Bauddha
      3. Avalokitesvara Shrines
         a. Jana Baha, Kathmandu
         b. Bunga Dya of Bungamati and Patan
         c. Chobar
         d. Nala
      4. Padmasambhava sites
      5. Jogini Shrines
      6. Namo Buddha, southeast of Dhulikhel
      7. Manichuda, north of Sankhu
   b. Valley seen as Buddhist country by the Tibetans, who also had a well-developed sense of the Valley's sacred places
   c. Newar Buddhist practitioners looked to as specialists sought for ritual teachings by neighboring mid-montane Tibeto- Burmese Buddhist groups

IV. Social Relations

A. Major Ethnic Groups
1. Newars
   a. half of population is agriculturalist
   b. long history of long-distance trade endures
   c. the richest ethnic group, per capita, in Nepal
   d. Tibeto-Burman dialect
   e. society divided according to Hindu and Buddhist castes
2. Paharis
   a. agriculturalists
   b. ruling elite
3. Nepalese Tibeto-Burmans and Tibetans
   a. Tamangs
      1. agriculturalists on Valley periphery
      2. seasonal laborers in towns and at peak agricultural seasons
   b. Sherpas in tourist industry, especially trekking
   c. Manangi and Thakali traders
4. Tibetan refugees
   a. live in special camps at Bauddha, Svayambhu, Patan; wealthy live in new suburbs around the Valley
   b. subsist mainly through trade and by employment in carpet weaving industry
   c. have sponsored revival of Tibetan Buddhist monasteries and customs in the Kathmandu Valley
   d. small Tibetan Muslim group

5. Indians
    a. wholesalers (Marwaris)
    b. petty traders
    c. pilgrims

B. Social Organization
1. Castes and ethnic groups typically divided into named sub-divisions associated with specific localities
2. Caste Societies: Newars, Paharis, and Indians
    a. kinship system is North Indian
        1. patrilineal descent, clan exogamy, preference for virilocal residence
        2. formal male dominance, with women retaining strong bonds to natal homes
        3. polygamy accepted, but rare
        4. Newar isogamous wedding pattern
        5. Territorial introversion a hallmark of Newar settlements
    b. Newar high caste division along Hindu-Buddhist lines
    c. *Brahman* ritualists as key figures
    d. common caste pattern: ideology of caste maintained, while former systems of inter-caste relationships weakens
3. Non-caste groups
    a. Tamangs
    b. Tibetan refugees
    c. Other Tibeto-Burman groups
4. Different ethnic groups have separate but overlapping ways of life

C. Political Relations
1. Dominant groups
    a. ruling Shah family
    b. nation-wide political elite in Kathmandu controls the modern state
    c. Newar cultural agenda prominent in Valley life
    d. major businessmen
2. Processes of social dominance
    a. Sanskritization as common process and mobility strategy
        1. especially powerful press to conformity in the capital
        2. royal participation and emulation
    b. business class wields power in society
    c. constituencies involved with foreign aid
3. Political articulation
    a. until 1990: "Partyless Panchayat System", with localities electing officials for local posts as well as to district and national assemblies

b. 1991: Elections to town and national government under multi-party system

c. student groups at Tribhuvan University and other colleges are active in national politics

d. Nepali Congress groups

e. independent newspapers

4. Sources of social conflict and resistence:

a. application of purity rankings and caste law

b. ethnicity as basis for political favoritism

c. efforts by Newars and others to preserve their own distinct languages and cultures

d. university policies among student population

V. Cultural Continuities

A. Major Languages

1. Newari
2. Nepali
3. Tamang
4. Tibetan

B. Religious Traditions

1. Hinduism

a. key domains of organization: temple institutions and Brahman networks

b. pantheon: Shiva-Pashupati, Vishnu, Ganesh, Devi, Krishna, Rama, Bhairav, Skanda, Indra

c. Brahmanical rituals

1. life cycle rites (*samskaras*)
2. *homa pujas*

d. religious life in the Valley is strongly affected by the state supported Hinduism:

1. observance of Hindu calendar
2. celebrations of *Dasain* and *Tihar*
3. royal patronage of shrines and their patterns of worship

e. tantric initiation and *guthi* membership define and reinforce high caste Newar Hindu status

2. Buddhism (Newar and Tibetan)

a. monastic institutions

1. *viharas*, maintained by a *sangha* of Newar Vajracarya and Sakya castes
2. Over 20 Tibetan *gompas* of Nyingma, Kargyu, and Gelug sects
3. Over 10 Theravada *viharas* (since 1950)

b. worship of *stupas*, especially Svayambhu

Pashupati Temple

Newar Buddhist Ancestor Ritual

        c. pantheon
            1. Buddhas
            2. Avalokitesvara
            3. Tara
            4. Vajrayana Yoginis
            5. Hariti Ajima
            6. Mahakala and other protectors
        d. major rituals
            1. *homa puja*
            2. *kalasha puja*
            3. life cycle rites (*samskaras*) [Newars only]
        e. patronage by merchant elites and refugee community
        f. esoteric initiations of tantric Buddhism define and reinforce
           high caste Newar status
    3. Indigenous oracle cult: the *Dya wa:mha*, mediums at regular shrines
       who undergo possession to heal, prognosticate, and preach ethical
       practices for all ethnic groups
    4. Relationship between Hinduism and Buddhism
        a. commonalities
            1. ancestor worship in families
            2. *puja* techniques and samskaras
            3. *ayurvedic* medical concepts
            4. lesser deities in the pantheon
            5. karma belief
        b. contrasts:
            1. major deities of the pantheon
            2. death rites
            3. festival observances
            4. priesthoods
            5. mythology

C. Cultural Processes and Continuities

    1. Sanskritization
        a. cultural processes all in this general direction, at least formally
        b. royal influence as exemplary patrons of Hindu cults and ritualism
        c. Buddhist Newars adopting *vajrayana* rituals in the Brahmanical
           style "sanskritize" their lifestyle to maintain cultural boundary
           vs. Hindu Newars rituals
    2. Tibetanization
        a. patronage of Tibetan refugee community strengthens the standing
           of the Kathmandu Valley as a center of Tibetan Buddhism
        b. influence confined to certain Newar Buddhists and other Tibeto-
           Burman Buddhist groups

3. Theravadin influences
    a. Sri Lankan and Burmese forms of celibate, monastic Buddhism, with emphasis on rationality of Buddhist doctrine, meditation, and lay practice
    b. confined mostly to the Newar community
4. Nationalization
    a. Shah state seeking to create a national polity, adapting local traditions, and using state machinery to extend their preferred socio-cultural norms
    b. as national capital and the seat of royal residence, the Valley is the chief center for political change and agitation
    c. direct access to the highest national courts and authorities has affected even the local communities that remain hardly aware of national events outside the Valley
5. Distinctive aspects of material culture
    a. dress, jewelry, and special foods are ethnic group markers
    b. Newar women never have pierced noses
    c. metal household and ritual utensils distinctive to Newars
    d. Newar houses and shop facades with highly crafted woodwork

Bhairav Temple, Bhaktapur

Recommended Readings and References

Allen, Michael. "Buddhism without Monks: The Vajrayana Religion of the Newars of the Kathmandu Valley," *South Asia* 3, 1973, 1-14.

Dowman, Keith. "A Buddhist Guide to the Power Places of the Kathmandu Valley," *Kailash* VIII (3-4), 1982, 183-291.

Gellner, David N. "Language, Caste, Religion and Territory: Newar Identity Ancient and Modern," *European Journal of Sociology* XXVII, 1986, 102-148.

_____. *Monk, Householder and Tantric Priest: Newar Buddhism and Its Hierarchy of Ritual*. Cambridge University Press, 1992.

Gellner, David N. and Quigley, Declan eds. *Contested Hierarchies: A Collaborative Ethnography of Caste among the Newars of the Kathmandu Valley, Nepal*. Oxford: Oxford University Press, 1995.

Gombo, Ugen. *Tibetan Refugees in the Kathmandu Valley: A Study in Socio-Political Change and Continuity and the Adaptation of a Population in Exile*. State University of New York at Stony Brook: Ph.D. Dissertation, 1985.

Gray, John N. "Domestic Enterprise and Social Relations in a Nepalese Village," *Contributions to Indian Sociology* 17 (2), 245-274.

Greenwold, Stephen M. "Buddhist Brahmins," *Archives Europeennes de Sociologie* XV, 1974, 483-503.

Iltis, Linda. *The Svasthani Vrata: Newar Women and Ritual in Nepal*. Ann Arbor: University Microfilms International, 1985.

Ishii, Hiroshi. "Institutional Change and Local Response," in Ishii *et al. Anthropological and Linguistic Studies of the Gandaki Area and Kathmandu Valley in Nepal*. Tokyo: Monumenta Serindica, 1986.

_____. "Social Change in a Newar Village," in N. Gutschow and A. Michaels eds. *Heritage of the Kathmandu Valley*, 1987, 333-354.

Levy, Robert. *Mesocosm*. Berkeley: University of California Press, 1990.

Lewis, Todd T. *The Tuladhars of Kathmandu: A Study of Buddhist Tradition in a Newar Merchant Community*. Ann Arbor: University Microfilms International, 1984.

_____. "Newars and Tibetans in the Kathmandu Valley: Ethnic Boundaries and Religious History," *Journal of Asian and African Studies* 38, 1989, 31-57.

Lienhard, Siegfried. "Nepal: The Survival of Indian Buddhism in a Himalayan Kingdom," in Heinz Bechert and Richard F. Gombrich eds. *The World of Buddhism*. New York: Facts on File, 1984, 108-114.

Locke, John K. *Buddhist Monasteries of Nepal*. Kathmandu: Sahiyogi, 1985.

_____. *Karunamaya*. Kathmandu: Sahiyogi, 1980.

_____. "The Vajrayana Buddhism in the Kathmandu Valley," *in The Buddhist Heritage of Nepal*. Kathmandu: Dharmodaya Sabba, 1986.

Macdonald, A.W. "A Little-read Guide to the Holy Places of Nepal," *Kailash* 3, 1975, 89-144.

Owens, Bruce. *The Politics of Divinity in the Kathmandu Valley: The Festival of Bunga Dya/Rato Matsyendranath*. Ann Arbor: University Microfilms International, 1989.

Parish, Steven. *Moral Knowing in a Hindu Sacred City*. New York: Columbia University Press, 1994.

Pradhan, Bina. *The Newar Town of Bulu*. Kathmandu: CEDA, 1982.

Quigley, Declan. "Introversion and Isogamy: Marriage Patterns of the Newars of Nepal," *Contributions to Indian Sociology* 20, 1986, 75-95.

Rosser, Colin. "Social Mobility in the Newar Caste System," in C. von Furer-Haimendorf ed. *Caste and Kin in Nepal, India and Ceylon*. Bombay: Asian Publishing House. 68-139.

Shakya, Min Bahadur. *A Short History of Buddhism in Nepal*. 2nd ed. Patan: Young Men's Buddhist Association, 1986.

Snellgrove, David. "Buddhism in Nepal," in *Indo-Tibetan Buddhism, Volume II*. Boston: Shambala, 1987, 362-380.

Toffin, Gerard. *Societe et Religion chez les Newar du Nepal*. Paris: CNRS, 1984.

_____. "Intercaste Relations in a Newar Community," in James Fisher ed. *Himalayan Anthropology*. The Hauge: Mouton, 1978.

Webster, Peter. "To Plough or not to Plough, a Newar Dilemma: Taboo and Technology in the Kathmandu Valley," *Pacific Viewpoint* 22, 1981, 99-131.

Witzel, Michael. "Meaningful Ritual : Vedic, Medieval, and Contemporary Concepts in the Nepalese Agnihotra Ritual," in A.W. van den Hoek *et al.* eds. *Ritual, State, and History in South Asia*. Leiden: E.J. Brill, 1992, 774-825.

PART V:

CONTINUITIES IN CULTURE, RELIGION, AND SOCIETY

Jagat Shumshere Rana and his Pandit, c. 1880

Tamang Lama

Chapter 16

FRONTIER VERSUS CORE CULTURAL PRACTICES
IN THE HIMALAYAS

I. Introduction

A. Frontier areas worldwide are known for their anomalous position in relation to related core culture areas

B. Peoples of the Himalayan region retain strong indigenous and autochthonous characteristics despite their "conversions" and incorporation into distant states

II. Indic Peoples

A. The social and religious order of North India has undergone considerable change in its migration to the hills.

B. Paharis are not entirely unique nor are they isolated from the rest of North India, but they still inhabit a distinct historical and cultural niche

C. Special distinctions:
1. Pahari language differs from other Indic languages
2. Smaller range of castes than is common in the plains with few *vaisya* and *sudra jatis*
3. Greater flexibility in intercaste relations; mixed marriages likely a vehicle of assimilating non-Indic peoples by dominant groups
4. Fewer prohibitions for women: less seclusion, easier divorce and remarriage
5. Except for the rich, mid-montane peoples do not conform to the plains ideal of joint family residence
6. High caste practices do not conform to *sastra* ideals:
    a. the prohibition against plowing
    b. eating meat
    c. drinking alcohol
    d. cross-caste marriages
    e. polyandry
    f. *brahmans* as exorcists
    g. bride price system instead of dowry
    h. fewer *samskara* rites observed

III. Tibetanized Peoples

A. Some peoples hunt and perform animal sacrifices, acts that conflict with Buddhist ethics; great lamas often make pilgrimages and exhort individuals to give up such observances

B. The monastic tradition in some areas is especially weak
1. Some married lamas do not perform the full spectrum of rituals from the Buddhist tradition
2. Local shamans or oracles occupy these "niches" in religious practice and draw from autochthonous traditions

C. In some areas, there is limited observance of central Tibetan festivals and conformity to Hindu practices

Recommended Readings and References

Berreman, Gerald. "Cultural Variability and Drift in the Himalayan Hills," *American Anthropologist* 62, 1960, 774-794.

_____. "Brahmans and Shamans in Pahari Religion," in Edward Harper ed. *Religion in South Asia*. Seattle: University of Washington Press, 1964, 53-69.

Ramble, Charles. "How Buddhist are Buddhist Communities? The Construction of Tradition in Two Lamaist Villages," *Journal of the Anthropological Society of Oxford* XXI (2), 1990, 185-184.

Mumford, Stan Royal. *Himalayan Dialogue: Tibetan Lamas and Gurung Shamans in Nepal*. Madison: University of Wisconsin Press, 1989.

Snellgrove, David. *Himalayan Pilgrimage*. Boulder: Prajna, 1981.

Newar Householder Vajracarya Priest

Gaine Minstrels, Central Nepal

Chapter 17

LANGUAGES IN THE HIMALAYAS

I. Introduction

A. Language is a central element in establishing a community's cultural identity and a fundamental feature of ethnicity

B. Many features of the Himalayan region have fostered the extremely complex pattern of linguistic diversity, even for South Asia where the Hindi proverb has it: "Every two miles the water changes and every four miles the dialect."

C. Distribution of ethnic group populations generally follow linguistic lines

D. Bi- and tri-lingualism a common trait

E. Difficulty of distinguishing firm line between "Tibetan" and some "Tibeto-Burman" languages

II. The Indic Family of Languages

A. All fall under the Indo-European language family and derive from ancient Sanskrit and Prakrits

B. "Dardic" Languages of the NW region
1. Kashmiri
2. Kohistani
3. Badrawali (Gaddi)

C. Plains languages spoken across the Submontane region
1. Punjabi
2. Dogri
3. Hindu-Urdu
4. Avadhi
5. Bhojpuri
6. Bihari
7. Maithili
8. Rajbangshi
9. Assamese

D. Pahari Languages
  1. Kangri
  2. Western Pahari (Garhwali)
  3. Central Pahari (Kumaoni)
  4. Eastern Pahari (Nepali; also called "*Khas kura*")

E. Tharu

III. Tibeto-Burman Languages

A. Some linguists posit a "Proto-Bodic" language from which Tibetan and Tibeto-Burman languages were derived

B. Indo-Nepalese Region
  1. Lahuli
  2. Spiti
  3. Byangsi
  4. Bura
  5. Magar
  6. Gurung
  7. Tamang
  8. Newari
  9. Sunuwari
  10. Rai
  11. Limbu
  12. Lepcha

C. Northeast Region
  1. Boro
  2. Monpa
  3. Dafla
  4. Aka
  5. Miri
  6. Abor (Adi)
  7. Garo
  8. Ahom
  9. Mishmi
  10. Mikir
  11. Dhimal

IV. Tibetan Languages

    A. Related historically to ancient classical Tibetan

    B. Western group, with relations with ancient Zhang-zhung language spoken on the upper Sutlej
1. Balti
2. Purig
3. Ladakhi

    C. Central group
1. Gtsang
2. Dbus
3. Thakali
4. Mustangi
5. Langthang
6. Sherpa
7. Walung

    D. Eastern Group
1. Dzongkha (Bhutanese)
2. Kham
3. Memba

V. Miscellaneous

    A. Munda Branch: Santal

    B. Dravidian

    C. Munda
1. Khasi
2. Malto

    D. As Yet Unclassified:
1. Burushaski (Hunza)
2. Kusunda (Nepal)

Recommended Readings and References

Bara, Mahendra. *The Evolution of Assamese Script*. Jorhat: Assam Sahitya Sabha, 1981.

Bhat, Roopkishen. *A Descriptive Study of Kashmiri*. Delhi: Amar Prakashan, 1987.

Dutta Baruah, P.N. *An Intensive Course in Assamese*. Mysore: Central Institute of Indian Languages, 1980.

Goswam, Upendranath. *An Introduction to Assamese*. Gauhati: Mani-manik Prakash, 1978.

Jarmul, Chamba. *A Nepali Newspaper Reader*. Kensington, Md.: Dunwoody Press, 1984.

Malla, Kamal P. *The Newari Language: A Working Outline*. Tokyo: Institute for the Study of Languages and Cultures of Asia and Africa, 1985.

Matthews, David. *A Course in Nepali*. London: SOAS, 1984; rev. ed. 1993.

Toba, Sueyoshi. *A Bibliography of Nepalese Languages and Linguistics*. Kathmandu: Linguistic Society of Nepal, Tribhuvan University, 1991.

Chapter 18

ETHNICITY AND ETHNONYMS

I. Introduction

A. Traditional ethnicity usually correlated closely with a home region and a distinctive subsistence lifestyle
   1. Castes and ethnic groups typically divided into named sub-divisions associated with specific localities
   2. If a faction moves and/or changes professions, it is likely that, over generations, this group will eventually change its name and assimiliate to its new home region

B. Maintenance of ethnic group boundaries
   1. Groups often have a stake in limiting interactions with outsiders and may benefit by maintaining their corporate solidarity
   2. Common element in socio-cultural traditions
   3. Exact in-group vs. non-group lines often in transition

C. Often modern names are merely modern neologisms adopted to unite culturally distinct peoples based upon state laws

D. In most cases, it is problematic to assume that names necessarily represent strict socio-cultural boundaries, historical continuities, or primoridal identities

E. A group may be diluted by new adherants until most of those in the group are not true descendants from original nucleus

F. The boundaries originally maintained by each ethnic group to preserve its identity lose their importance in circumstances where, together, these groups make up a legally demarcated distinct minority

G. Modern state efforts to impose singular cultural identity and official languages have led to mixed results:
   1. Schooling and government services have weakened minority language study and comprehension by new generations
   2. Such policies have motivated certain minority leaders of ethnic groups formerly isolated (and hardly related) to unify in order to address their grievances

3. Often, leaders of such communities had to rely on the lingua franca they oppose to communicate

H. Many ethnic groups have other names from their own dialects that they use to refer to themselves

II. Factors Affecting Ethnic Names

A. Certain peoples changed their names in order to adapt to the socio-cultural exigencies of political rule

B. "Martial caste" names were adopted by individuals in order to secure employment in the Indian, Gurkha and/or British armies

C. Many ethnic groups have formal "social committees" that define their group/caste identity and regulate behavior in local and state relationships

D. Nepal's *Muluki Ain* and the Rana state imposed some standardization

E. Migrants and traders known for adopting multiple ethnic codes and names to interact successfully to new locations

III. Major examples

A. The name "Tamang" was extended to many Tibetanized peoples in the twentieth century as a result of a Rana decree that united various Tibetanized groups of the central mid-montane area, especially "Murmi", "Lama", etc.

B. The name "Thakali" was adopted by Tibeto-Burman language speaking groups in the upper Gandaki watershed as part of an elite's strategy to claim "Rajput" status and gain favorable treatment in trade from the Shah state

C. The modern "Rai" of eastern Nepal
   1. Really more than ten groups that speak mutually unintelligible dialects
   2. Seem to have adopted their single ethnic name which in Nepali was used simply for designating leaders of villages or local descent groups
   3. Groups became aware of their common bonds by adopting new name

D. The modern "Limbu" people of eastern Nepal possibly acquired their name from "*Eka Thomba*", a general Pahari term for people of their region

E. The Sherpas of Nepal
   1. Once "Sherpa" ("Easterners") designated only the highland residents of the Solu-Khumbu/Mt. Everest region
   2. In the last century, highlanders of Helambu, an highland area adjacent to and northeast of the Kathmandu Valley, began using this term to refer to themselves
   3. Tibetans from many other points now adopt the name to gain employment as mountaineers and guides

F. Humla Tibetans now refer to themselves as "Tamang"

G. "Newar" has little ethnic precision and derives from the name that merely indicated a resident of the Kathmandu Valley, i.e., "Nepa"

H. Gurungs who migrated to Sikkim changed their name to "Khas"

I. The "Lepchas" call themselves "Rong-pa"

Recommended Readings and References

Burghart, Richard. "The Formation of the Concept of Nation-State in Nepal," *Journal of Asian Studies* XLIV, 1, 1984, 101-125.

Gellner, David N. "Language, Caste, Religion and Territory: Newar Identity Ancient and Modern," *European Journal of Sociology* XXVII, 1986, 102-148.

Hofer, Andras. *The Caste Hierarchy and State in Nepal: A Study of the Muluki Ain of 1854*. Innsbruck: Universitatsverlag Wagner, 1979.

Holmberg, David. "Ritual Paradoxes in Nepal: Comparative Perspectives on Tamang Religion," *Journal of Asian Studies* 43 (4), 1984, 697-722.

Levine, Nancy. "Caste, State, and Ethnic Boundaries in Nepal," *Journal of Asian Studies* 46 (1), 1987, 71-88.

Oppitz, Michael. "Myths and Facts: Reconsidering Some Data Concerning the Clan History of the Sherpa," in C. von Furer-Haimendorf ed. *Contributions to the Anthropology of Nepal*. Warminster: Aris and Philips, 1974, 232-243.

Yogin living in a rock shelter, Pashupati

Chapter 19

SPIRIT POSESSION IN THE HIMALAYAS

I. Introduction

    A. Spirit possession, one of the continuities in world religions, a common feature in the religious life of the Himalayan region

    B. A vehicle by which normal individuals and, most commonly, cultural specialists communicate with divinities

    C. A common idiom whereby individuals objectify illnesses and the community orchestrates a collective, healing response

    D. Practitioners closely associated with use of a vast array of amulets that they empower and give to laymen

    E. Specialists often associated with symbols and rituals expressive of ethnic group identities

    F. Sometimes elements of these traditions conflict with Brahmanical or Buddhist norms and are supported by non-elite groups

II. Roles Associated with Spirit Possession in the Himalayas:

    A. The Afflicted-Possessed
        1. Ordinary individuals who are possessed by demons or evil local deities
        2. A culturally-defined and approved means for the resolution of inner conflicts, especially in melding personal desires with conflicting cultural norms

    B. Shaman/Exorcists
        1. Shamanism similiar cross-regionally: with the aid of a tutelary deity, individuals make "spirit flights" and/or become possessed to diagnose diseases and prescribe cures
        2. Their role is often to objectify a patient's illness in terms of foreign substances or divine/demonic affliction
        3. A prestigious role, especially for low status individuals who are virtually excluded from important religious positions in caste societies
        4. Teacher-pupil transmission of techniques/teachings is central and may cross ethnic group lines

5. Examples:
   a. *Dehar*, among the Kalash peoples of Pakistan
   b. *Jhankri*, in Nepal
   c. Tamang *Bonpo*
   d. Tharu *bharara*
   e. *jane manche* in Nuvakot region, Nepal
   f. Rai and Limbu shamans who lead the dead to proper dwelling places
   g. *baki* of Garhwal hills

Newar Masked Dancer

C. Mediums/Oracles
   1. Individuals associated with fixed shrines at which they enter into trance
      states
         a. At prominent temples
         b. In Jumla, at Khotan shrines
   2. Activities
         a. prognostication
         b. subduing demons, witches, ghosts
         c. preaching devotion to patron deities and the importance of
            ethical behavior
   3. Often the mediumship role will remain in family lineages
   4. Examples:
         a. oracle *lamas* of Ladakh
         b. *dhamis* of NW Nepal who are possessed by the "*Masta* Deities"
         c. *dya wamha* of the Newars
         d. Newar masked dancers
         e. *lhawa* of the Sherpas
         f. Tamang *lambu*
         g. Lepcha *pano*

Rai *Jhankri*

D. The Child as Incarnate Deity
1. Newar examples from the Kathmandu Valley
    a. *Kumaris*: young girls in the Newar community who are selected to serve as incarnations of goddesses until they reach puberty
    b. *Kumars*: young men from certain select castes dance as particular deities for ceremonial occasions connected to the tantric cults of the former royal palace
2. Gurung girls dance as goddesses in the yearly *Ghanto* festival and are the focal point of elaborate ritualism
3. Young girls called "*Kumaris*" receive offerings on certain dates at the Kamakhya temple, Assam

E. Priesthoods
1. Lamas and Newar *Vajracaryas*: members of the Buddhist priesthood who take on the "divine egos" of high gods in the pantheon during the *sadhana* in the *vajrayana* rituals
2. *Brahman* exorcists who undergo possession in Uttar Pradesh, western Nepal
3. Gurung *kepre*, although not possessed, heals clients, controls demons, leads in clan worship of deities, and prepares souls for travel to the ancestral realm after death

Kathmandu Royal *Kumari*

Recommended Readings and References

Campbell, J. Gabriel. *Consultations with Himalayan Gods: A Study of Oracular Religion and Alternative Values in Hindu Jumla*. Ann Arbor: University Microfilms International, 1977.

Fanger, Allen C. "The Jagar-Spirit Possession Seance among the Rajputs and Silpakars of Kumaon," in Maheshwar P. Joshi, Allen C. Fanger, and Charles W. Brown eds. *Himalaya: Past and Present*. Almora: Shree Almora Book Depot, 1990.

Fürer-Haimendorf, Christoph von. "Himalayan Religions," in Mircea Eliade ed. *The Encyclopaedia of Religion* (Volume 6) 1987, 325-329.

Hitchcock, John and Jones, Rex eds. *Spirit Possession in the Nepal Himalayas*. New Delhi: Vikas, 1976.

Maskarinec, Gregory G. "A Shamanic Semantic Plurality: Dhamis and Jhankris of Western Nepal," in M. Hoppal and O.J. von Sandovszky eds. *Shamanism: Past and Present*. Fullerton: Istor Books, 1989.

Michailovsky, Boyd and Sagant, Phillippe. "The Shaman and the Ghosts of Unnatural Death: On the Efficacy of a Ritual," *Diogenes* 158, 1992, 19-37.

Miller, Caspar J. *Faith Healers in the Himalayas*. Kathmandu: Center for Nepal and Asian Studies, 1979.

Mumford, Stan Royal. *Himalayan Dialogue: Tibetan Lamas and Gurung Shamans in Nepal*. Madison: University of Wisconsin Press, 1989.

Nebesky-Wojkowitz, R.M. *Oracles and Demons of Tibet*. The Hague: Mouton, 1956.

Samuel, Geoffrey. "Shamanism, Bon and Tibetan Religion," in Charles Ramble and Martin Brauen eds. *Anthropology of Tibet and the Himalayas*. Zurich: Volkerkundemuseum, 1993.

Sidky, M.H. "Shamans and Mountain Spirits in Hunza," *Asian Folklore Studies* LIII, 1994, 67-96.

Stablein, William. "A Descriptive Analysis of the Content of Nepalese Buddhist Pujas as a Medical-Cultural System," in James Fisher ed. *Himalayan Anthropology*. The Hague: Mouton, 1978, 403-411.

Watters, David E. "Siberian Shamanistic Traditions Among the Kham Magars of Nepal," *Contributions to Nepalese Studies* 2, 1975, 123-68.

Kailash Volume 9, 1982: Special issue on death rituals

Chapter 20

MIGRATION STRATEGIES AND THE REMITTENCE ECONOMY

I. Introduction

    A. A common action in the subsistence strategies of mid-montane Himalayan peoples is for men (and sometimes women) to migrate out of the home area to earn cash; their remittences are essential in support of the household

    B. An ethnic group's socio-cultural traditions and political connections shape distinctive patterns of cross- regional network building and migration

    C. High caste Pahari groups have succeeded better than Tibeto-Burman peoples at building regional alliance networks

    D. Highland peoples have the greatest tendency to engage in trade and semi-nomadic pursuits as part of their subsistance strategies

II. Seasonal Migration

    A. Cash earning on short-term basis in lumbering, road- building projects, petty trade

    B. Simple vacancy: in areas where the local land can only support a limited number of people, individuals leave in the cold season to subsist elsewhere

III. Year-long Migration

    A. Securing jobs in a hill city, e.g. Kathmandu or Dehra Dun, or in the plains, returning home for holidays, special family events, perhaps peak agricultural seasons

    B. The population in residence in many hill areas for most of the year consists of women, children, the elderly

Magar Worker in Tibetan Carpet Factory, Pokhara

IV. Longer term migration

A. Military service or settlement overseas, with only scattered visits to the hills before retirement
   1. British Gurkha regiments
   2. Indian army

228

B. Nepalis working in the Indian Himalayas on road crews and as seasonal laborers

C. Upon retirement, individuals often return to the home village

D. Prostitution slavery

V. Permanent Migration

A. With the eradication of malaria in some places, mid- montane groups have settled in the formerly sparsely populated Terai regions of Nepal, an area that has been a "safety valve" for that country's population explosion
   1. Example of Chitwan, Nepal:
      a. 1955 population: 40,000
      b. 1971 population: 183,000

B. Indian peoples of Bengal and Bangladesh have moved into Assam and Arunachal Pradesh

C. Nepali herders have settled across the eastern Himalayan region, including highland Burma

Recommended Readings and References

Bishop, Naomi H. "Circular Migration and Families: A Yolmo Sherpa Example," *South Asia Bulletin* XIII(1-2), 1993, 59-66.

Fricke, Thomas E. *Himalayan Households: Tamang Demography and Domestic Processes.* New York: Columbia University Press, 1994.

Gaige, Frederick H. *Regionalism and Nationalism in Nepal.* Berkeley: University of California Press, 1975.

Parry, Jonathan. *Caste and Kinship in Kangra.* Boston: Routledge and Kegan Paul, 1979.

Peet, Robert Creighton. *Migration, Culture, and Community: A Case Study of Rural Nepal.* Ann Arbor: University Microfilms International, 1978.

Seddon, D. Blaike, P and Cameron, J. *Peasants and Workers in Nepal.* Warminster, England: Aris and Phillips, 1979.

Leh Bazaar, Ladakh

Chapter 21

PATTERNS OF PAN - REGIONAL CHANGE

I. Introduction

    A. Beneath the apparent contrasts between the "traditional" and the "modern" in rural communities lie the continuing uniformities of inequality, political dominance, and ongoing communal relations

    B. Modern change takes place on interlocking levels; the effects are multi-directional and often unforeseen by the peoples affected and their governments

    C. Individual biographies as well as familiy and settlement histories all reveal the extent to which people are in constant adaptation, continually re-assessing their situation according to their state laws, resources, kin, connections, wealth, and cultural values

    D. Long-term observers are struck at the speed of change in many areas

II. Modern Trends in Subsistence Practices

    A. Hill Agriculture
        1. Intensifying existing crops, but retaining subsistence orientation
        2. Increasing the land under cultivation
        3. Increasing the practice of employing paid laborers
        4. Adapting plantings to new market structures introduced by roads
        5. Adopting new hybrid seeds

    B. Pastoralism
        1. Highland peoples increasing the use of cross-breed cattle which cannot live at higher elevations
        2. Greater herds on highland pasture lands, animal overpopulation in certain areas
        3. Increased use of pack animals by traders
        4. Strains on older systems that regulated highland communities' use of resources
        5. With the decline in polyandry, increased partition of highland estates leading to smaller, less viable holdings
        6. Gujjar herders now found further east in Uttar Pradesh

Lopped Trees, Terai

C. General shifting of mid-montane people from emphasis on herding to greater reliance on fixed agriculture

D. Widely reported sense of subsistence farmers feeling their life becoming more precarious

E. Rising land prices in many areas

III. Environmental Crises

A. Overpopulation
1. Birth rate has increased
2. Modern medicine has increased the longievity rate
3. Malarial eradication has been a fundamental factor promoting quickly expanding settlement in the submontane region

4. Typical pattern: there are three times the number of people living in the same place as lived there in 1850

B. Marginal land recently terraced and farmed leading to increasing soil erosion, landslides, siltification of rivers

C. Overgrazing by animals and excess fodder cutting

D. In certain areas, forests cut down or in retreat due to firewood and fodder cutting, overgrazing

E. Growing dependence on chemical fertillizers

F. Many species of wild animals in danger of extinction

Mid-Montane Domestic Scene, Eastern Nepal

IV. Roads and Transport

A. Radically transforming the socio-economic networks
   1. The introduction of mass-produced consumer goods often has undermined local cottage industries
   2. Roads have made access to the plains easier and quicker, expanding wage-earning, migration, and pilgrimage options
   3. In places, roads have encouraged farmers to reorient their crops and husbandry toward newly accessible markets

B. More rapid and direct introduction of outside influences in every field of human endeavor
   1. Birth control devices
   2. Medicines
   3. Mechanized agricultural tools
   4. Photography

Monsoon Landslide, Central Nepal

234

5. Radio cassettes
6. Video cassettes and mass media
7. Satellite dishes

V. Urban Areas

A. Rapid growth of cities
   1. Mainly through in-migration as the carrying capacity of rural lands is exceeded and migrants move in
   2. Formation of towns around bureaucratic enclaves
      a. expansion of governmental services
      b. development of industrial sites
      c. growth of transport entrepots

B. Problems in maintaining minimum urban services, especially electricity, sewage treatment, medical facilities

C. Persistent inability to alleviate poverty and malnutrition among the poorest urban dwellers

D. Educational systems creating more graduates than the state systems can employ

VI. Political Trends

A. Patterns of internal colonization: elites in modern states exploiting the remaining venues of mountain resources for private gain

B. Regional nationalistic movements by minority castes and ethnic groups seeking to resist socio-cultural assimilation and exploitation by outsiders

C. Democracy movements in Nepal and Bhutan

VII. Modern State-Sponsored Development Projects

A. Seek to solve unfolding problems at greatest possible speed

B. Early efforts introduce modern technologies: electricity, roads, ropeways, water systems, transport

C. Effective in alleviating crisis situations

Political Posters, Nepal

D. Recurring problems:
   1. Inappropriate technology
   2. Failures in long-term planning and management
   3. Corruption
   4. Failures in performance undermine society's faith in state-run projects implemented by outsiders

VIII. Increasing diversity of migration patterns and subsistence strategies within population groups as they adapt to changes induced by all the above factors

A. Strains in sustaining former community bonds

B. Difficulties in modern states creating unified multi-ethnic polities

IX. Some Demographical and Socio-Economic Indicators, 1991

A. Nepal-Bhutan Comparison

	Nepal	Bhutan
1. Population	19.5 Million	1.5 Million
2. Pop. growth	2.3 %	2.3 %
3. Infant mortality /1,000 births	118	118
4. Literacy	20.7 %	18.0 %
5. People per Doctor	20,356	9,791
6. People per Telephone	686	684
7. GNP	$170	$ 190
8. GDP Growth	2 %	9 %
9. Exports/yr	$ 0.2 billion	$ 0.07 billion
10. Foreign debt	$1.5 billion	$ 0.07 billion
11. Official Inflation rate	11.5 %	8.8 %

(Source: *Asiaweek* statistical profile, 7/19/91; Figures are available only for nations.)

B. India Population Figures:
1. Jammu and Kashmir: 7,718,700
2. Himachal Pradesh: 5,111,079
3. Sikkim: 403,612
4. Assam: 22,294,562
5. Arunachal Pradesh: 858,392
6. Meghalaya: 1,760,626
7. Pan-India population growth rate: 2.1 %
   (Source: Indian Census Report, 1991)

X. The Future

A. Population explosion and environmental degradation

B. Increased spread of modern market economy

C Increased state presence in all domains of life, rural and urban

D. Continuing influence of Indian culture and Hinduism

E. Continued demographic movement into submontane region

F. Ethnic identity and boundary maintenance recurring themes in group political movements

G. Decline in traditional cultural observances

H. Increasing influence of English

I. Expansion of international communications

Community Trail Repair, Thak Khola, Nepal

Recommended Readings

Berreman, Gerald D. "Identity Definition, Assertion and Politicization in the Central Himalayas," in Anita Jacobson-Widding ed. *Identity: Personal and Socio-Cultural.* Atlantic Highlands: Humanities Press, 1983, 289-317.

Bista, Dor Bahadur. *Fatalism and Development.* Calcutta: Orient Longman, 1991.

Crook, John H. "Buddhist Ethics and the Problem of Ethnic Minorities: The Case of Ladakh," from Charles Wei-hsun Fu and Sandra A. Wawrytko eds. *Buddhist Ethics and Modern Society.* New York: Greenwood Press, 1991, 229-245.

Dodin, Thiery. "Ecumenism in Contemporary Ladakhi Buddhism," in Per Kvaerne ed. *Tibetan Studies, Volume 1.* Oslo, 1994, 168-177.

Eckholm, Eric. *Losing Ground: Environmental Stress and World Food Problems.* New York: Norton, 1976.

Fisher, James F. *Sherpas: Reflections on Change in Himalayan Nepal.* Berkeley: University of California, 1989.

Forbes, Ann Armbrecht. *Settlements of Hope: An Account of Tibetan Refugees in Nepal.* Boston: Cultural Survival Report 31, 1989.

Hausler, Sabine. "Community Forestry, A Critical Assessment: The Case of Nepal," *The Ecologist* 23 (3), 1993, 84-90.

Ives, J.D. and Messerli, B. *The Himalayan Dilemma: Reconciling Development and Conservation.* New York: Routledge, 1989.

Justice, Judith. *Policies, Plans, and People: Foreign Aid and Health Development.* Berkeley: University of California Press, 1986.

Karan, Pradyumna P. and Iijima, Shigeru. *Bhutan: Development Amid Environmental amd Cultural Preservation.* Tokyo: Institute for the Study of the Languages and Cultures of Asia and Africa, 1987.

Karan, Pradyumna P. and Ishii, Hiroshi *et al* eds. *Nepal: Development and Change in a Landlocked Himalayan Kingdom.* Tokyo: Institute for the Study of the Languages and Cultures of Asia and Africa, 1994.

Mullin, Chris and Phuntsog Wangyal. *The Tibetans: Two Perspectives on Tibetan-Chinese Relations.* London: Minority Rights Group #49, 1983.

Norberg-Hodge, Helena. *Ancient Futures: Learning from Ladakh.* San Francisco: Sierra Club, 1991.

Pigg, Stacy Leigh. "Inventing Social Categories through Place: Social Representations and Development in Nepal," *Comparative Studies in Society and History* 34, 1992, 491-513.

Sarin, Vic. *India's Northeast in Flames*. New Delhi: Vikas, 1980.

Shepherd, Mark. "Chipko: North India's Tree Huggers," *The Coevolution Quarterly*, Fall 1981, 62-70.

Tuting, Ludmilla and Dixit, Kunda. *Bikas-Binas/Development-Destruction: Change in Life and Environment of the Himalaya*. Kathmandu: Modern Printing Press, 1986.

Zaman, M.Q. "Crisis in the Chittagong Hill Tracts: Ethnicity and Integration," *Economic and Political Weekly* 17 (3), 1982, 75-80.

Zurick, David N. "Traditional Knowledge and Conservation as a Basis for Development in a West Nepal Village," *Mountain Research and Development* 10 (1), 1990, 23-33.

Two publications are also noteworthy for their coverage of ongoing environmental news in the Himalayas: *Mountain Research and Development* and *Himal*

Kathmandu, 1987